Twayne's English Authors Series

Sylvia E. Bowman, *Editor*

INDIANA UNIVERSITY

Doris Lessing

 (TEAS) 21

Doris Lessing

By DOROTHY BREWSTER

Columbia University
(Retired)

Twayne Publishers, Inc.   ::   New York

Library of Congress Catalog Card Number: 65–18222

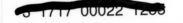

With this book the author pays tribute to Barnard College on the occasion of its 75th anniversary

Preface

Since the conspicuous success in 1950 of her first novel, *The Grass Is Singing*, Doris Lessing, of English parentage and Rhodesian upbringing, has been recognized as one of the most gifted of the younger group of English novelists. She left Salisbury to live in London in 1949, and since that time both the Rhodesias, Northern and Southern, and Nyasaland, briefly united in a Federation that has failed, have been undergoing the rapid changes associated with the breakup of the colonial system and the emergence of the new African states. Those of Doris Lessing's novels and stories that deal with the people and ways of life of Southern Rhodesia before, during, and after World War II have acquired something of the significance of social and political history. They illumine aspects of that past out of which the present is being painfully shaped. When she came to London, she looked at the English—known to her hitherto only through her own family and the white colonial Rhodesians—with an alert and fresh vision that makes her narrative, *In Pursuit of the English*, one of the most delightful of her books.

The first chapter of this study is biographical, based upon her own statements and upon pertinent material from her writings, with the purpose of suggesting the ties between her experience and her fiction. The following chapters discuss the themes and technique of her first novel and four of the novelettes with Rhodesian settings; the more than fifty short stories—a form of which she has had the mastery from the beginning; a novel with an English setting, *Retreat to Innocence*, and four novels in the series entitled *Children of Violence*, to be completed eventually by a fifth; and finally the long novel, *The Golden Notebook*, in which for the first time

Mrs. Lessing has experimented in a notable way with form. This much-discussed novel raises more questions in several different fields—artistic form, politics, feminism, sex—than it answers; and the discussion focuses mainly on the questions. "The novel," as one of the characters in the book says, "has become a function of the fragmented society, the fragmented consciousness," and the discussion may seem fragmented, but, I hope, provocative.

Literary influences upon Doris Lessing's work, wherever I have found them interesting or significant, or she herself has referred to them, are mentioned in context. Of her two published plays, only one is treated at length; but her interest in the theater is keen and will certainly lead her further into the writing of plays. She is a writer in mid-career. This study is written in the hope of making the wide range and high artistic merit of her work better known to a wider reading public.

My thanks are due to Mrs. Lessing for letting me read the typescript of her forthcoming novel, *Landlocked,* and for permission to quote from her published works.

DOROTHY BREWSTER

New York City
October, 1964

Contents

Chronology

The dates in this chronology are chiefly those of the publication of Doris Lessing's books and the performances of her plays. Details are included in the bibliography.

1919   Doris Lessing born in Kermanshah, Persia. Daughter of Alfred Cook Tayler, born in Colchester, Essex, England, and of Emily McVeigh, born in London.

1925   Family moved to Southern Rhodesia, Africa, and settled upon a farm in the district of Banket.

1949   Doris Lessing went to London, where she has made her home. Until she was fourteen, she had attended a convent school in Salisbury, the capital of Southern Rhodesia. After several years on the farm, she went to Salisbury, earning her living in various ways, chiefly in secretarial positions. She married twice, both marriages ending in divorce. Lessing is the name of her second husband.

1950   *The Grass Is Singing.*

1951   *This Was the Old Chief's Country.*

1952   *Martha Quest.*

1953   *Five.*

1954   *A Proper Marriage.* Received the Somerset Maugham Award, Society of Authors, for *Five.*

1956   Visited Rhodesia, and on her return was proclaimed a prohibited immigrant, apparently because of unacceptable views on the color question. *Retreat to Innocence.*

1957   *The Habit of Loving. Going Home.*

1958   *A Ripple from the Storm.* Play, *Each His Own Wilderness,* performed at the Royal Court Theatre, London.

1959   *Fourteen Poems.*

1960   *In Pursuit of the English.*

1962   *The Golden Notebook. Play with a Tiger,* a play, pro-
        duced and published in London.
1963   *A Man and Two Women.*
1964   *African Stories.*
1964   Reissue of *Martha Quest,* as vol. I, and *A Proper Mar-
        riage,* as vol. II, of the series which will include five
        novels, with the over-all title, *Children of Violence.* Mac-
        Gibbon & Kee, London, have bought from Michael
        Joseph, London, the rights to *Martha Quest, A Proper
        Marriage,* and *A Ripple from the Storm,* and will pub-
        lish (1965) the first two novels in one volume, and *A
        Ripple from the Storm* separately. They will publish
        Landlocked in June, 1965. Simon and Schuster have sold
        Children of Violence to The New American Library of
        World Literature, Inc. (New York).*
1965   *Landlocked.*

* Information in a letter from Doris Lessing to Dorothy Brewster,
April 13, 1965, from London.

CHAPTER 1

Biography

I *An African Childhood*

WHEN novelists use their own experience—and when do they not?—in writing of the growth and development of fictional heroes and heroines, and when we have facts about their own lives from various sources, readers inevitably make comparisons and draw conclusions. Sometimes the author will help us out, not necessarily by telling the truth, but at least what has come to seem to him the truth. Any inveterate reader of novels and biographies could elaborate on this theme, any reader of Tolstoy, Proust, Dickens, Joyce, Thomas Wolfe, but why run down the list? What did they do with their fathers and mothers, their grandmothers and brothers, not to mention themselves? The young woman named Martha Quest in the series *Children of Violence* grows up, like her creator, Doris Lessing, on a farm in Central Africa, has a father and a mother with some traits resembling those ascribed elsewhere by Doris Lessing to her own father and mother, goes at eighteen or so to earn her living in the capital of the colony, as Doris Lessing went to Salisbury, and is there shocked and stimulated by new ideas and new relationships in the rapidly changing conditions of the years before and during World War II. We must assume that Mrs. Lessing, in tracing Martha's development, has not forgotten her own.

Mr. Quest and Mrs. Quest, Martha's father and mother, the family Martha tries, with partial success, to escape from, are characters in their own right; and they live in many scenes that are surely imagined, not remembered. Mrs. Lessing has told us about her own father and mother, but we can see how Mr. and Mrs. Quest, resembling them, took their own development in hand, once they were launched.

Mrs. Lessing contributed to a series about fathers in the

London *Daily Telegraph* an article reprinted in *Vogue*, February 15, 1964. "I knew him," she writes of her father, Alfred Cook Tayler, "when his best years were over." After a country childhood in Essex, he became a bank clerk in the town of Luton, having a rather happy time for ten years until the outbreak of World War I, in which he served as an officer. Convalescing from the amputation of a leg in the Royal Free Hospital in London, he met the nurse whom he married in 1919. His war memories, writes his daughter, were "congealed in stories that he told again and again . . . in stereotyped phrases." Mr. Quest also talks of the war, and he shares with Mrs. Lessing's father the sense of disillusionment and betrayal in "the war to end war." After Mr. Tayler's marriage, he took a position in the Imperial Bank of Persia, first in Kermanshah, where Doris and her younger brother were born, and then in Teheran, where the social life was lively and there were musical circles. It was pleasant for his wife, who, like her fictional prototype, Mrs. Quest, was a musician. But Mr. Tayler was not so happy. An honorable man, he resented some corrupt practices that he discovered around him. It was always in the name of honesty or decency, writes his daughter, that he "refused to take this step or that out of the slow decay of the family's fortunes."

In 1925, going on leave to England, he took his family overland through Russia; and on the basis of that journey, as Mrs. Lessing says, her parents were both "experts for ever on the subject of international communism." There was an Empire Exhibition in London. Farming in Rhodesia seemed a very prosperous enterprise. Mr. Tayler bought a large farm and transported his family, a governess, and all the family possessions, including a piano and Persian rugs, to the high veld of Southern Rhodesia. The farm was a couple of hundred miles south from the Zambesi River, a hundred miles or so from Mozambique. There was gold in the region, and the farms produced vast crops of tobacco and maize. It was wild country, but coming more and more under cultivation. The Africans had been turned off the land and settled in Reserves, from which of course the farmers drew their labor. The neighbors—English, Scotch, Welsh, and (later comers) Afrikaans from the south—lived at distances of four to seven miles away.

The Taylers built a thatched house on top of a kopje, a small hill overlooking in all directions a "great system of mountains, rivers, and valleys, under a great arched sky." During the next few years, there was more bad luck than good—not the worst kind of luck, such as ruins the Turners in Mrs. Lessing's first novel, *The Grass Is Singing*, but bad enough: crop failures, veld fires, plagues of locusts, falling prices. Mrs. Tayler had a period of neurotic illness, then recovered and became brave and resourceful. Her husband withdrew more and more into a world of his own, dreaming of getting off the farm through some miracle of finding a gold mine or receiving a legacy, and experimenting with all sorts of theories, such as finding gold through divining rods using the attraction and repulsion of metals.

The short novel, *Eldorado*, portrays such a dreamer in a family setting but with a development quite different from that of Mrs. Lessing's family. But the dreamer, Mrs. Lessing told me, is drawn from her father. Mr. Tayler had many fanciful and misanthropic ideas, and had illnesses both real and imaginary, but he was a kind man, when he emerged from his preoccupations. In Mr. Quest we have a person whose remoteness and whose kindness are both brought out in scenes, sometimes humorous and sometimes moving, with his wife and daughter. Mr. Tayler, like Mr. Quest, liked to sit outside his door at night, smoking, watching the sky and the mountains: "In the dry season, the great dark hollow of night was lit by veld fires; the mountains burned through September and October in chains of red fire."

Mrs. Lessing writes, in her book *In Pursuit of the English,* that she didn't understand her father until she had been in England for some time. She recalls how he used to sit in his deck chair, surveying those leagues of African landscape, and now and then shaking his fist at the sky and shouting, "Mad—everyone—everywhere!" She had thought some of his ideas pathological until she found them merging easily into the local English scene. As for her mother, she was an intrinsically efficient mixture of English, Scotch, and Irish, and she did not furnish the clues Mr. Tayler did to the oddities of the English. At one point in Martha Quest's meditations, when dissatisfied with the particular shell she is living in, she wonders about the shells her father and mother inhabited before they came to Africa. There was her father's childhood in the English country village—honest simplicity with the bones of the house showing through lathe plaster; outside, a green and lush country, but tame, tamed. That would not suit her. Or, to dip into the other stream that fed her blood: "a tall, narrow Victorian house, crammed with heavy dark furniture, buttoned and puffed and stuffed and padded, an atmosphere of things unsaid." Martha on one occasion notices her mother's thickened clumsy hands and remembers how beautiful they once were, and how once, lying in the dark at the farm, listening to the piano several rooms away, she had gone to the doorway and seen her mother sitting at the keyboard, "a heavy knot of hair weighting her head and glistening gold where the light touched it from two candle flames." A Chopin nocturne "rippled out into the African night, steadily accompanied by the crickets and the blood-thudding of the tom-toms from the compound."

Both England and Persia lived on in Mrs. Tayler's memory, and bloomed in the garden of a South African home in the little story Doris Lessing wrote, entitled "Flavors of Exile," told in the first person by a young girl, whose mother had devoted an acre of rich soil near the house to a flourishing vegetable garden: "rich chocolate earth studded with emerald green, frothed with the white of cauliflowers, jeweled with the purple globes of eggplant and the scarlet wealth of tomatoes. Around the fence grew lemons, pawpaws, bananas—shapes of gold and yellow in their patterns of green." But the precious water had to be brought up from the well, and water was gold; and the garden was finally allowed to become overgrown with wild and vagrant plants, among them some Cape gooseberries that made delicious jam. But they were not English gooseberries—"if I could let you taste a pie made of real English gooseberries!" The girl's mother yearned for Brussels sprouts, and raised a few bitter little cabbages, shared with her neighbors from Home and politely accepted by her daughter and her Scotch neighbor's young son William. The little girl's awakening emotions centered on William, and this first love grew with the growth of a pomegranate tree which her mother, remembering roses and jasmine and walnut trees in

Persia, had planted—the only one of four which survived. In Persia pomegranate juice "ran in rivers." It was a small thorny tree, producing rusty red fruit with small seeds and bitter juice. The children shared the seeds and the mother's memories of pomegranate juice, drunk with melted snow from the mountains.

The little girl's fantasies about William—a tactful boy who pretended to enjoy things, to please older people, and who had clear eyes like water over gray pebbles—sustain her while another ugly little fruit slowly ripens on the tree. She dreams of William's finding her among pomegranate trees, and she can hear the sound of his grave voice "mingled with the tinkle of camel bells and the splashing of falling water." She nurses the fantasy in William's absence, and so the fantasy of early love and the ripening of the fruit run their course together. When the fruit is ripe, she has her mother invite the MacGregors to tea to celebrate; and William goes with her to the tree. When he knocks the fruit off, it explodes in a "scatter of crimson seeds, fermenting juice, and black ants." He looks at the seeds, and at her (with a warning she has seen in his eyes before—he is three years older), and says, "There's your pomegranate; we'd better go up if we want any tea." And she in a "bright careless voice" announces to the grownups, "It was bad, after all; the ants had got at it."

Revisiting Rhodesia in 1956, after an absence of seven years, Mrs. Lessing (in *Going Home*, pp. 33-52) recalls scenes of her childhood, in "the big mud-walled grass-roofed house on the kopje where the winds came battering and sweeping, and where I would fall asleep to the sound of my mother's playing Chopin and Grieg two rooms off, against the persistent thudding of the tom-toms from the native village down the hill." And she would imagine the people in the compound dancing around the big fire: "The drums beat through all the nights of my childhood; stronger even than the frogs and the crickets." During twenty years (1936-1956) she had lived in over sixty different houses, flats, and rented rooms; but she had never felt at home since she had left that first house on the kopje. It had crumbled long ago, but she rebuilds it in her memory, as she flies on this return journey over Salisbury, on a magnificent night: "the Southern Cross on a slant overhead; the moon a clear, small pewter; the stars all recognizable and close. The long grass stood all around tall, and giving off its dry, sweetish smell, and full of talking crickets. The flattened trees of the high veld were low above the grass, low and a dull silver-green."

The house was made of mud dug from the big antheaps, the best for the walls, blended as it has been by the jaws of a myriad of workers. Sometimes there are difficulties, as when skeletons are uncovered so laid out that it is clear they are the bones of chiefs, with earthen cooking pots beside them, and white meal mingled with the earth, and then the builders refuse to go on, fearing the spirits of their ancestors. But some of the earth had already been pounded into mud. "So the walls of our house had in them the flesh and blood of the people of the country." Step by step Mrs. Lessing, with her gift for the most precise concrete detail, describes the building and roofing and thatching of the house. A house like this is "a living thing, responsive to every mood of the weather"; and, during the time she was growing up, it had already begun to sink back into the forms of the bush. "I remember it as a rather old, shaggy animal standing still among the trees, lifting its head to look out over the vleis and valleys to the mountains." A poem, "The House at Night," picks up that image:

> The house grew there, self-compact;
> And with what long hopeless love
> I walked about, about—
> To make the creature out.

She was writing about a group of suburban town houses—"a herd of houses"—but could not have written about them had she not been brought up in the house she is describing:

> Till suddenly a mocking light
> Flashed on from that one house I'd searched,
> As if a beast had raised
> His head from where he grazed.

Looking from the windows of her own room in that house, she seemed on a level with the circling mountains, on a level with the hawks which wheeled over the fields. From her open doorway she could see the great chrome mountain ten miles off. The field of maize below the house changed its patterns and colors with the seasons. She could see in the field the Afrikander oxen with their long snaky horns and watch flocks of guinea fowl moving out of the bush at dawn and sunset, seeking the hidden seeds. And there was the drama of the coming of the rain, showers and storms, advancing and retreating, like storms at sea; and in the intervals between showers, when the winds were strong, "the whole field swayed and moved like a tide coming in."

Equally absorbing was what went on in her room: "For after a decade or so of weathering, the house had become the home of a dozen kinds of creatures not human, who lived for the most part in the thatch of the roof. Rats, mice, lizards, spiders and beetles, and once or twice snakes, moved through the thatch and behind the walls." However fascinated by these creatures, she always examined the bed carefully before tucking herself in under the mosquito net, where nothing could fall on her from the roof or crawl over her in the dark. In the wet season frogs pattered over the floor. She knew the map of the walls. Little holes near the roof housed hornets. "And if the wall was in a continual state of disintegration and repair, an irregular variegated surface of infinite interest, then the floor was not at all the flat and even surface of convention." A young tree used to shoot up under her bed every wet season, where there was a crack in the mud, be cut down, and reappear next season. Once she let it grow; it pushed up against the mattress and she thought it would be "attractive to have a tree growing in the middle of my bedroom," but her mother didn't agree. Next season it came up at the side near the wall, with a watch clutched in its leaves—like a Dali painting. It seems that her father had a theory about the folly of buying expensive watches, only to have them lost or stolen, so he bought a dozen turnip watches at five shillings each. They never broke, and one fell into the crack in the mud floor and came up in the arms of the tree.

White ants were a constant threat, and the antheaps could be from ten to twenty feet high. "After the rains, a grass-

covered peak of earth which has looked dead will suddenly
sprout up an extra foot or so overnight of red granulated
earth, like the turrets and pinnacles of a child's fairy castle." In
the walls of the house the ants made red galleries, like branch-
ing arteries. After the family left the house empty in the bush,
the ants conquered. Ant hills grew in the rooms, and finally
came a fire from the bush and all was destroyed. Returning
years later, Mrs. Lessing wanted to drive through the bush to
the kopje, but did not. She used to dream of the collapse
and decay of the house and of the fire, and she deliberately
sought to dream it all back—setting herself as she was going
to sleep to recover every detail of this or that room, or of a
certain tree, or a turn in the road. Over the months she recovered it all; "and so what was lost and buried in my mind, I recovered from my mind; so I suppose there is no need to go
back and see what exists clearly, in every detail, for so long as
I live."

In a house like that, Martha Quest grows up; and many
characters, particularly young girls and boys, in Mrs. Lessing's
short novels and stories, belong to that region of farms on the
high veld.

Children on those vast farms had to be sent away to school,
the boys usually to the better schools, often to the Cape. Doris
went to a convent school in Salisbury, but was as unhappy
away from home as Emily Brontë exiled from the Yorkshire
moors. She left school at fourteen. Returning to Salisbury in
1956, she met several of her old school friends, but their exchange of memories tells us little of those years. When Doris at
about eighteen left the farm to make her living in Salisbury,
she had a head full of ideas gained from extensive reading.
Certainly her Martha Quest comes to town with that equipment: Martha, whom we see first sitting on the veranda
steps, reading a popular science book, but with Havelock Ellis
open beside her. She is fifteen, and has had her reading en-
couraged by the Cohen brothers, whose father owns the general store at the railroad station, that "little clutch of corrugated iron-roofed buildings, a couple of stores, the garage,
the post-office, the station-master's house," where the farmers
congregated on their various errands, where the mealie sacks

used to be piled up waiting for the train to come to carry them off to Salisbury to market. The station and all that went on there are very important in the story of Martha Quest's childhood. Mrs. Lessing, on that return visit, found it changed, with a new hotel.

At the time of this visit she had already published two volumes of the *Children of Violence* series, covering the years of Martha's childhood, girlhood, and first marriage; her first novel, *The Grass Is Singing;* and two collections of her short stories. She had become known for her opinions on African problems; and, in fact, as she found out after she had returned to London and had been formally prohibited from entering South and Central Africa, she had been made a prohibited immigrant years before. "We only let her in this time," said an official to whom a relative of hers in Southern Rhodesia had been talking at a party, "by accident." She was cheered by this Alice-in-Wonderland inefficiency, "the one respect in which Central Africa is superior to the Union."

Going Home is a personal narrative: partly a travel notebook, partly a writer's diary including material for short stories, partly a journalist's day-by-day comments and interpretations, partly recollections of her life on the farm and in Salisbury. In noting the changes, political and social, that had occurred in Salisbury during her absence, she is an excellent journalist, using incidents and conversations carefully selected to reveal typical attitudes toward the problems of a color-bar society. She had left in 1949 before the establishment of the Federation of Northern and Southern Rhodesia and Nyasaland; and she found on her return that the question constantly coming up in conversation was "How is Federation working?" History has given the answer in 1964: it did not work. Northern Rhodesia and Nyasaland have achieved independence, under the names of Zambia and Malawi. Southern Rhodesia is one of the big trouble spots on a troubled continent.

Mrs. Lessing found in 1956, among all the shifting social, industrial, and political changes, that the "stale patterns of white domination" were as prominent as ever. It is of how these patterns concern her as a writer that she writes most significantly.

In an article in the *New Statesman,* April 21, 1956, "Being

Prohibited," Mrs. Lessing writes: "A large number of my friends are locked out of countries and unable to return; locked into countries and unable to get out; have been deported, prohibited and banned. Among this select company I can now hold up my head." Before planning her trip to the Union of South Africa and Rhodesia, she had wondered whether she would be let in. But what, after all, had she done to the Union government? In 1947 she had worked for a newspaper —the *Guardian*—in Cape Town for two months as a typist. The paper was in a permanent financial crisis, and she wrote many letters for the finance committee. On her way through South Africa to England in 1949, "I undeniably consorted with people since named as communists. Some were, some were not." It was no secret that she had joined the Communist Party in England, and some of her friends thought she was mad to expect to be let in; but others laughed at that. Wasn't she on the official list of South African authors at South Africa House? However, she was ordered out of South Africa after an official had telephoned to Pretoria. She expected to find the Southern Rhodesian atmosphere good-humored, compared to that of the territories north and south, but she was actually followed about all the time of her visit by the political police. Still, she got around. She visited a native compound on a Rhodesian tobacco farm, inspected factories employing native workers, listened to welfare workers and native schoolteachers, anthropologists, white trade union leaders, talked off the record with the Prime Minister of the Federation (who had been her mother's doctor), visited the Copper Belt in Northern Rhodesia, and spent an evening at an adult night school for natives who worked all day in the town.

Revisiting Rhodesia after the years of literary success in London made Mrs. Lessing wonder whether she must go on writing about the "stale patterns of white domination" that still existed. She had notebooks full of stories, plots, anecdotes, which at one time or another she had felt impelled to write. "It is always the color bar; one cannot write truthfully about Africa without describing it. And if one has been at great pains to choose a theme which is more general, people are so struck by the enormity and ugliness of the color prejudices which must be shown in it that what one has tried to say gets lost."

Among her favorite novelists are the nineteenth-century
Russians—Tolstoy, Dostoevsky, Chekhov, Turgenev; so a comparison comes readily to her mind. White-settler Africa in
many ways resembles the Russia of *Anna Karenina,* with its
landowners and peasants. "I am struck continually by the
parallels between Pre-revolutionary Russia . . . and that part
of Africa I know. An enormous, under-populated, unformed
country, still agricultural in feeling and resisting industrializa-
tion." Discussions and soul-searchings about the peasant in
the Russian novels are paralleled in Rhodesia by endless talk
about the natives, who, like the Russian peasants, are considered by the white landowner-liberal as lazy, irresponsible,
shiftless, superstitious. Like Tolstoy's Levin, this landowner
in Africa is decent and worried, drawn to the native, but cannot trust him to govern himself. "For a novelist based on Africa,
it is discouraging that so much of what develops there is a
repetition of the European nineteenth century." A writer
seizes a theme, realizes he will repeat what has been said in
another context, tries to isolate what is peculiarly African,
and comes up against that "complex of emotions, the colour
bar." Here is a company of peoples, diverse, original, varied,
but only after they are free, can they find out what they are.
So the writer is always finding the complexity and richness, nar-
rowing down to a protest against "that monstrous thing, the
colour bar." (*Going Home,* pp. 19-21.)

Reminders of nineteenth-century Russia belong to the past,
and to literary memories. But as she talked with old friends,
as she drove along the comfortable streets of her home town,
past the pretty houses with their patios, gardens, and servants,
she understood suddenly and for the first time that "this was
an American small town"—familiar from a hundred films. She
had not realized this likeness before, because Southern Rhodesia was so self-consciously British, even though the British
had become a minority even among the white people, the
Afrikaners, Greeks, Italians, and so on. But the society was becoming American in the sense that people were judged by
how much they earned; there was no class feeling, only money
feeling. "It is a society without roots—is that why it has no
resistance to Americanism?" "The myths of this society are
not European. They are of the frontiersman and the lone-wolf;

the brave white woman home-making in lonely and primitive conditions; the child who gets himself an education and so a status beyond his parents; the simple and brave savage defeated after gallant fighting on both sides; the childlike and lovable servant; the devoted welfare worker spending his or her life uplifting backward peoples." Yet she goes on to demonstrate that these images "have no longer anything to do with what is now going on in Central Africa."

On her shopping expedition she found many changes. Not merely Coca-Cola signs everywhere—even in the "scruffy little store in the Native Reserve"—but refrigerated counters, self-service shops—all very different from the pictures we get from her early stories, or from *Martha Quest* and *A Proper Marriage,* dated before and during World War II. The main street is crammed with cars, with white women drifting along, talking, well-dressed, women of leisure; and, having been one of them—"or at least expected to play the role of one" —Doris Lessing knows the order of their preoccupations: "the dress they are making for themselves or their daughter; the laziness of their servants; and an infinite number of personal problems." And she knows that their husbands are busy getting on in their offices, the children are at school, the cookboy is preparing the lunch, they are filling the car with groceries and liquor and bargains, there will be a morning tea-party (and that is *not* American)—and then lunch, a nap, afternoon tea, and soon "sundowners"—in our idiom, cocktail parties before dinner.

A school friend is among the women. They talk, and the friend hopes she is going back to write "something nice about us for a change." Sitting on the pavement, their feet comfortably in the gutter, are five African women, knitting, relaxed and happy, watching life go by. Their clothes have changed for the better in a decade: good print dresses, sandals, crocheted white caps; no more of the old blue-printed cottons, worn like a uniform. The days of "Kaffir-truck," she is told, are over, and cheap bright stuff is imported for the native trade, but soon the natives will be buying as good quality as the Europeans. (58-60)

And so she goes on noting the changes, never losing sight for long of the color problem. After one particularly vivid picture of native living conditions, she quotes an official concerned with health, to the effect that the mainstay of white supremacy is not the police, it is the sun; "the only reason they get away with these dreadful conditions they make the natives live in, is that the sunlight makes life tolerable." (174) Here are living quarters in a township: "Looking through a doorway into the two minute rooms like large dog-kennels, at the rolled sleeping blankets, the cooking pots, the tin plates, a sack of grain or a sieve of groundnuts, one imagines oneself standing in a village in the bush, looking into the doorway of a traditional hut." (167)

II   *Discovering the English*

In Pursuit of the English, a personal narrative like *Going Home,* but shaped like a novel, was not published until 1960. But Mrs. Lessing entered upon the pursuit in 1949, when she left Rhodesia for the first time. Why at that time? Because, she says, of her propensity to do things the hard way; and in 1949 England was at its dingiest and her personal fortunes at their lowest and her morale at zero. And she had a small son, the child of her second marriage, which had ended in divorce. Cape Town, where she had to wait until she could arrange transportation, was the first stage of the pursuit—or of the initiation—the Cape being definitely English. And the account of her days there and of the people she met is in her best vein of lively observation and reportage. How London first affected her is recalled in a passage in *Going Home:*

It was a nightmare city I lived in for a year; endless miles of heavy, damp, dead building on a dead, sour earth, inhabited by pale, mis-shapen, sunless creatures under a low sky of grey vapour. Then, one evening, walking across the park, the light welded buildings, trees and scarlet buses into something familiar and beautiful, and I knew myself to be at home. Now London is to me the pleasantest of cities, full of the most friendly and companionable people. . . . It is the variegated light of London which creates it; at night, the mauvish wet illumination of the city sky; or the pattern of black shadow-leaves on a wall; or, when the sun emerges, the instant gaiety of a pavement.

But when she was back in Africa, it was "my air, my land-scape, and above all, my sun." (12)

Mrs. Lessing brought with her to London the manuscript of her first novel, *The Grass Is Singing*. She had written and destroyed six novels, according to a brief biographical note prefaced to her article in *Declaration*. *The Grass Is Singing* was promptly accepted and published, received highly favorable reviews, and was reprinted seven times within five months. *This Was the Old Chief's Country*, a collection of ten stories with African settings, followed in 1951. She found lodgings in a house with a rich assortment of fellow tenants, and they and the surrounding neighborhood gave her an insight into some very lively aspects of London life.

It is amusing to read some of the reviews that greeted *In Pursuit of the English*. "A particular kind of floating London life"; "socially it already belongs to the past"—both from *The Manchester Guardian*[1]—"rather untypical people in a rather untypical house" (cautious verdict from the *New Statesman*);[2] "sub-Dickensian" (*Sunday Times*);[3] "slightly shady proletariat," remarks Marvin Mudrick in the American quarterly *Hudson Review*,[4] and goes on to say that the author is "determined to admire her lower classes, including their money-grubbing, drunkenness, shiftlessness, cruelty, nymphomania, prudery, and such staple British meals as beans on toast with chips and spaghetti as well as to detest that mythical country America, because her iron political bias instructs her to." The iron political bias and the detestation of America are themselves mythical.

Richard Findlater in the *Evening Standard*[5] is accurate and understanding, noting that her housemates were not exactly typical figures. But, he goes on, "their attitudes to sex, food, work and money are full of illuminating clues to some of those patterns and etiquettes of behavior that make up the elusive, undefinable English way of life." A happy comparison is used by Jean Ware in the Liverpool *Daily Post*[6]: "The intimacy of this piece of writing is forced on the reader in the same way as the insides of London lodging houses were brutally revealed to our unwilling gaze during the Blitz, in all the pathos and struggle of everyday living, caught unawares." *John O'London's*[7] rightly calls it a "minor masterpiece of observation."

The fortunes of the people in the house have their ups and downs, climaxes and resolutions, and are involved with some outsiders; and there is a court action at the end over an eviction that deserves to be called Dickensian without any "sub" prefixed. Most of the characters are in on it and the most interesting of them all—Rose—puts legal intricacies into a plain prose that is devastating. When the lawyer is trying to get the couple in the basement—Flo and Dan—to tell consistent stories, and is getting nowhere, Rose says: "Now listen, what you've got to do is to tell the same lies at the same time." And again, "All this law business isn't anything to do with right and wrong, see? You'll just get everybody confused if you start thinking so silly. Nobody cares what really happened."

Winning the case brings about a revolution, and the whole place is restored to livability. Dan and Flo acquire a television set. Flo (of Italian origin) stops making her great Italian Sunday dinners, and they and their friends sit with plates on their laps watching "Telly." Flo disposes of the puppies that used to be under foot and soon the basement is inhabited by Flo, her dreadful, pathetic child Aurora ("Oar"), a single sleep-drugged cat, and the television screen. The new generation slips in at the end in the person of Rose's young brother—released from reform school—and his friend, who watch television and carry on an absurd sort of backchat as nonsensical as the famous Cockney rhymes—about "mutated mink," a "furry little animal called haggis," and other private jokes picked up from the movies and the television. Rose and Flo and the older people just don't get it; they are puzzled and rather sad. Another instance of the younger generation knocking at the door! It is Rose, who works in a shop, who directs Mrs. Lessing to the lodging house, where she herself lives, and who undertakes to show her about. "You don't mind me saying it dear, but you don't know how to look after yourself." The streets and shops come alive under Rose's guidance. House-hunting alone had been a dreary business: "interminable streets of tall, grey, narrow houses that became half-effaced with fog at a distance of a hundred yards, the pale faces peering up from basements, past rubbish cans, the innumerable dim flights of stairs, rooms crowded with cushioned and buttoned furniture, railings too grimy to touch . . . above all, an atmosphere of stale weariness." (41)

Where was this house? Reviewers guess in the neighbor-hood of Notting Hill, or Paddington, or Bayswater. Such houses can still be found among the increasingly numerous blocks of Council flats. It is one in a row of tall old houses damaged by the blitz; opposite, a cliff of gray flats, with jut-ting balconies hung with greenery and flowers, each with an old lady peering down into the street, knitting, screeching when she sees the kids in danger among lorries and cars. Dan, an enterprising fellow who had served in the navy, bought the house and rented out the rooms, but he couldn't get rid of an old couple who had lived there during the blitz in sur-roundings of filth and couldn't be thrown out because of the Rent Act—until at the end Dan brought the lawsuit and won.

The second object of Mrs. Lessing's pursuit in England was the working class, and she was now housed in a working-class quarter. "Working-class" is not too easily identified, as any-one will agree who has ever wandered about the high streets and side streets and cul-de-sacs of this or that borough in the vast city. And Doris Lessing did just that, by herself, or under the protective guidance of Rose, or the very dubious chaper-onage of the "con" man, Bobby Brent—or Ponsonby—or Mc-Namara—he had several names and histories to go with them —who offered to find her lodgings at the start, and who con-tinued to pop up with new schemes to get her money. Dan and Bobby worked together in a housing racket. Bobby found his victim naïve enough at the beginning, but she learned his ways and, to his reluctant admiration, turned the tables on him at the end, puncturing a little scheme of his to involve her in a literary-libel skin-game. He is as corrupt as they come, but rather appealing, with his air of "Please let me trick you; please let me cheat you; I've got to: it's essential for me." A writer as curious about people as Mrs. Lessing cannot help being amused and fascinated, even to her own cost.

But about the working class. She had been told that she must, if she would write, "become pervaded by the cultural values of the working-class"; the Africans, she was told, were not working class but "semi-urbanized peasants." Nor were the tenants and people in the neighborhood the proper subjects of her study; they may have worked with their hands, but they were the "lumpen proletariat, tainted by petit-bourgeois ideology." Even miners and members of the Labor Party and trade unionists did not qualify, she was told. The entire working class of England had become tainted by capitalism and had lost its teeth. She was advised to go to Africa, where "the black masses are not yet corrupted by industrialism" (all except the semi-urbanized peasants, no doubt). (13-14)

Mrs. Lessing was, by her experience, equipped to play with comparative anthropology. Workmen from some war-damage bureau come to her attic room to do something about the dangerous cracks in the walls, and they take about a month to do the job; she, meanwhile, is working at her typewriter. They all drink tea; the foreman discusses the Labour Government, and agrees that they could do the job in half a morning. They are highly and humorously articulate, and very kind. They carry coal up for her, they always sweep up the dirt, they drink more tea. And Mrs. Lessing watches them work—when they do—and feels homesick, for she comes from a country of "accomplished idling." There is the memory, perhaps, "of a black labourer, hoe in hand, commanded to dig over a flower bed. . . . He saunters out, hoe over his shoulder. He lets the hoe fall of its own weight into the soil and rest there, till, with a lazy lift of the shoulders, the hoe rises again, falls . . . the man stands thinking." A shout of rage comes from the house, but he makes no sign of hearing. Then the hoe rises and falls again. "Leaning on the handle, he gazes into the distance, thinking of that lost paradise, the tribal village, where he might be lounging at that moment, under a tree, watching his women work in the vegetable garden while he drinks beer." Another shout from the house: "What do you think I pay your wages for?" The answer is in the sullen set of the shoulders: "So that I can pay that stupid tax and get back home to my family." (222-23) We note, by the way, the feminist viewpoint contained within the sympathy for the native who is forced to work for the white man. What about the women, black or white?—a dominant theme in Doris Lessing's work.

That attic room, with sounds coming up through the old house—a tap dripping, a wireless playing—makes her think of an anthill: "a tall sharp peak of baked earth that seems abandoned, but which sounds, when one puts one's ear to it, with a continuous vibrant humming." (86)

This is a London still badly scarred by the war and still in the grip of austerity, and memories are fresh. Rose remembers the six years of hardship as a period of warmth and comradeship, when she had a feeling of belonging, of being wanted, such as she had not had before or since. "She could talk about the war for hours and never mention death, fear, food shortages or danger." Mrs. Lessing may very well be largely indebted to Rose for making us believe in some of the experiences and attitudes of the woman named Rose in the short novel, *The Other Woman*—the only story in the collection *Five* that has an English setting. Both Roses have similar opinions about politics. The Rose in the lodging house, though she didn't believe in any of Churchill's ideas, used to take a "dreamy pleasure" in listening to his speeches on the wireless. She is a virgin, and a cautious one, although she is not without suitors to take her out evenings. But it is only after a long time that she is sure enough of one of them to let him in for the night. And after that experience of love, she reproaches Doris (who is her confidant) for not letting her know how nice it was. "But we did let you know," she is reminded. "Well, I suppose no one can properly tell in words about it, but if I'd known what I was missing, I wouldn't have held out so long." Many modern novelists, one sometimes regrets, persist in trying to tell about it in words.

Miss Privet, a professional, spends a few weeks in the lodging house, convalescing from an illness; during some talks with the author, she expresses opinions about sex quite different from Rose's. In answer to the question whether she doesn't want to get married to one of the gentlemen in her life, she replies: "The way I look at it is this. You get bored with one man, don't you? You get just as bored with four. So you might as well settle for one." Asked if she doesn't ever like sex, she is offended: "if you're going to talk dirty, I'm not interested . . . I can't stand dirty talk. Never could." Miss Privet took Doris walking one evening about sunset, after a wet day, and they stood at the entrance to the National Gallery and looked out over Trafalgar Square. It was one of those "bright intervals" that figure so hopefully in English

weather forecasts. The bells were rolling from St. Martin-in-the-
Fields. There was "a soft glistening light falling through a low
golden sky. Dusk was gathering along walls, behind pillars
and balustrades. The starlings squealed overhead. The buildings along Pall Mall seemed to float, reflecting soft blues and
greens on to a wet and shining pavement. The fat buses, their
scarlet softened, their hardness dissolved in mist, came rolling
gently along beneath us, disembarking a race of creatures
clad in light, with burnished hair and glittering clothes. It was
a city of light I stood in, a city of bright phantoms." (230-31)
Miss Privet had a print of Monet's "Charing Cross Bridge" in
her room. "That's London," she said, "but you have to learn
to look."

Doris Lessing had learned to look.

III   *Dreams and Declarations*

So there was Africa and then there was England. Doris Lessing, dreaming through her Martha Quest, often visited a particular region of sleep which Martha called "that country."
" 'That country' was pale, misted, flat; gulls cried like children around violet-coloured shores. She stood on coloured
chalky rocks with a bitter sea washing around her feet and the
smell of salt was strong in her nostrils." Well, thought Martha,
waking from one such dream, I suppose it is England, "but
how can I be an exile from England when it has nothing to
do with me?"

Dropping back to sleep again, she found herself standing at
the edge of Mr. McFarline's gold-eating pit. (A Mr. Macintosh
and his pit figure in the novelette *The Antheap*.) But in the
dream it had been abandoned centuries before; the enormous
gulf "had been worked by a forgotten race which she saw
clearly in her dream: a copper-coloured, long-limbed, sharp-
featured people, tied together like slaves under the whip of a
black overseer. Centuries ago these people had vanished," and
the pit sides were covered with low bushes and rank grass.
Near where she stood, there was a projection into the pit, "a
jut of layered rock that spread at its base, like a firmly set
animal's foot." Smelling the hot African sun on the loose dry
soil, she examined fold after fold of the deep-layered rock,

a warm red showing the living soil at the top, then the subterranean dead layers of rock beneath. She saw that the projection into the pit was not dead, but living. It was not an animal's paw, but the head and shoulders of an immense lizard, an extinct saurian that had been imprisoned a thousand ages ago, in the rock. It was petrified. The shape of the narrow head, the swell of the shoulders, was visible. A narrow ledge of rock along the grass-grown bottom of the pit was its dead foot. Martha looked again and saw that its eye was steadily regarding her with a sullen and patient query. It was a scaly ancient eye, filmed over with mine dust, a sorrowful eye. It's alive, she thought. It's alive after so many centuries. And it will take centuries more to die. Perhaps I can dig it out? (A *Ripple from the Storm*, 101-102)

The dream of England (Doris-Martha's) is later replaced by the sharp reality of the London of Mrs. Lessing's *Golden Notebook* and the stories with English settings. So far as she can be considered an exile now, she is an exile from Africa. The imagery of this fascinating dream suggests the powerful hold Africa has upon Mrs. Lessing's imagination—an eye steadily regarding her, with a question demanding an answer.

Dreaming, for Mrs. Lessing, seems to be something of a discipline—as when she recreated in memory the house on the veld. Once in Cape Town, on a holiday, as she stood on a hill looking over the city and the sea, she watched mist come creeping over the scene, blotting out everything. Later it would come back to her as a dream of destruction, along with the dream of the heap of red sinking earth and dead grass with the trees growing through it: "I first restored the house, and then forced the mist back, rolled it back off the city and the sea and the lighted ships and back through the gap in the mountains. It took a long time, but at last the city was free and illuminated again." (*Going Home*, 51-52)

The questions demanding answers were becoming more insistent during the years of Mrs. Lessing's life in Salisbury. When she looked back from England, and created Martha Quest to live through the decades of the 1930's and 1940's, she raised the political as well as the personal problems, for Martha was a very active girl. It would be treading on dangerous ground to take Martha's views on politics to be Mrs. Lessing's, no mat-

ter how broadly similar her experience must be considered to
be. But Mrs. Lessing can be quoted in her own right. She
takes the opportunity in *Going Home* to state her opinion that
a writer should not become involved in day-to-day politics:
"The evidence of the last thirty years seems to me to prove
that it has a disastrous effect on writing." But she herself, she
admits, does not stick to this principle because a puritan sense
of duty drives her out to meetings which she knows are a
waste of time, as well as to others which are not, but would be
better assisted by someone else; and also because she finds
"political behavior inexhaustibly fascinating." "Nevertheless
I am not a political agitator. I am an agitator manquée," who
sublimates that side of her personality by mixing with people
who are. (55-56) Martha plays the role (of agitator manquée)
with a mixture of enthusiasm and misgiving that is fully por-
trayed in *A Ripple from the Storm*.

In 1957 Mrs. Lessing contributed to *Declaration,* a collection
of "separate positions" by eight of the leading younger writers in England, a statement entitled "The Small Personal
Voice" about the novel and the novelist. A brief introductory
biographical note tells us that from 1943 she was busy politically "taking her first lessons from Communists and Socialists
in the R.A.F." Her first teachers in fiction were the great
nineteenth-century novelists: Tolstoy, Stendhal, Dostoevsky,
Balzac, Turgenev, Chekhov—the Realists; and Realism to her
means the art that springs "so vigorously and naturally from a
strongly held, though not necessarily intellectually defined
view of life, that it absorbs symbolism." These writers had in
common "a climate of ethical judgment"; they shared certain
values; they were humanists. But today in our literature, with
the confusion of standards and the uncertainty of values, the
great words like *love, hate, loyalty, treachery,* and the rest,
"contain their opposite meanings and half a dozen shades of
dubious implication." "Words have become so inadequate to
express the richness of our experience that the simplest sentence overheard on a bus reverberates like words shouted
against a cliff."

When she rereads the giants—and it is cheering to hear that
most of the people she knows do that—she is not looking for

reaffirmation of old ethical values, many of which she no longer accepts; but she is looking for the warmth, the compassion, the humanity, the love of people, which illuminate the literature of the nineteenth century and make these old novels a statement of belief in man himself. That is the "commitment" in which she believes. And, even after fifteen years of uncomfortable adjustment to reality, she still finds herself in "the possession of an optimism about the future obviously considered jejune by anyone under the age of thirty." Commitment to her does not mean being a propagandist for a political party or policy or line; yet she does not rule out the possibility that the passion with which a writer is committed in that sense may, if he has talent, make literature of the propaganda.

She is of course acutely conscious of the dangerous world created by the explosion of the atom, one facing us with a great nightmare but also with a great dream. Artists are "the traditional interpreters of dreams and nightmares." They have the choice of presenting an evil or strengthening a vision of the good that may defeat the evil—or of doing both? It is very difficult to imagine the freedom—the free man—of the possible future: "Slaves imagining freedom see it through the eyes of slaves." But we either force ourselves to make the effort of the imagination needed to become what we are capable of being, or submit to being ruled by "the office-boys of big business, or the socialist bureaucrats who have forgotten that socialism means a desire for goodness and compassion, and the end of submission is that we shall blow ourselves up." The really frightening figure in our world to Mrs. Lessing is not the madman pushing the button, but rather the "young empty-faced technician in anonymous overalls, saying 'Yes, sir.'" There is, as we all know, a "terrible gap between the public and the private conscience, and . . . until we bridge it we will never be safe from the murderous madman or the anonymous technician."

Oversimplifying more than a little, she looks at two sides of the coin of contemporary literary production: from the socialist countries, a literature optimistic, jolly, and curiously unemotional; and on the other side, despairing statements of emotional anarchy. "One sees man as the isolated individual unable to communicate, helpless and solitary; the other as collective man with a collective conscience." The resting point between "should be the writer's recognition of man, the responsible individual, voluntarily submitting his will to the collective, but never finally; and insisting on making his own personal and private judgments before every act of submission."

She sees the basic ethical conflict of Communism to be between what is due to the collective and what to the individual conscience. Outward pressures are an easily recognized danger, but more dangerous to the individual conscience is that inner loyalty to something felt as greater than one's self. She remembers, in Moscow, discussing these problems with a well-known Soviet writer who felt that there were times when humanity is so pitiful and so exposed that art should be willing to stand aside and wait for life. Mrs. Lessing argued that there is a point where committedness of this sort can sell out to expediency.

Turning to her own work, she declares herself concerned in her series of novels entitled *Children of Violence* with a study of the individual conscience in its relations with the collective. She has been disturbed by the indifference of the younger generation—the twenty-year-olds—to such great movements as the Chinese and the Russian revolutions and to "all that sort of thing—progress and all that is rather old hat." One young woman had said that she envied her because for ten years she had believed in the purity of Communism. "It is true," Mrs. Lessing comments, "that when I became a Communist emotionally, if not organizationally, in 1942, my picture of socialism as developed in the Soviet Union was, to say the least, inaccurate." But she reaffirms her optimism and concludes that, if an artist has once felt that he is caught up in a great whirlwind of change and has made the effort imaginatively to comprehend it, "it is an end of despair and the aridity of self-pity."

It will be interesting to see how her theories work out in her fiction, and particularly in *The Golden Notebook*.

CHAPTER 2

Early Fiction

I   *The Grass Is Singing*

*T*he Grass Is Singing takes its title from *The Waste Land*, from the passage picturing the decayed hole among the mountains, where the grass is singing over the tumbled graves, and the empty chapel, windowless, with swinging door, is only the wind's home. The quotation is placed before the first chapter as an epigraph; and the desolation of the lines forecasts the ruin that overtakes the Turners and their house on the veld. The passage ends with a threatening image: "the jungle crouched, humped in silence . . . then spoke the thunder." This promises a grim and even a terrifying story, and the promise is fulfilled in what was immediately recognized as a remarkable first novel. But there is another brief epigraph, "author unknown," which contains another promise, and that promise, too, is carried out: "It is by the failures and misfits of a civilization that one can best judge its weaknesses."

Dick and Mary Turner were very ordinary people, certainly no candidates for tragedy, who might have lived out their ordinary lives separately, he on his substandard farm in the South African colony, and she in the town as an efficient secretary, who did not get married young like others of her set at the girls' club, and so began to seem a little ridiculous to her contemporaries as she grew older. Her life would have been dull but not disastrous. Unfortunately, she met Dick on one of his trips to town; they blundered into marriage; and she went to live on the farm in a miserable little box of a house, which Dick was always going to add to or improve, but never had the money even to roof properly to protect them from the blistering heat. They saw nobody but the African farm laborers, who lived in the native compound, and the houseboys, who came and went, because Mary, having had no experience with servants, treated them in accordance with fixed ideas about their shiftlessness and dishonesty, and so they never stayed long. Their nearest neighbors, five miles away, the ruthless Charlie Slattery and his wife, made friendly overtures; but they did not persist in the face of Mary's coldness. Mary felt ashamed of the poverty of her house, and yet superior because of her experience in the social life of the town. Others thought her "stuck-up!" Even with exchange of visits, big family parties at this farm or that, frequent sundowners, and trips to the store at the railway station, the women on the isolated farms had a lonely time. But they usually had children. The Turners felt they couldn't afford children until they were able to send them to decent schools, and that time never came.

So for six years this ingrown life of frustration and poverty and isolation went on. Dick worked his land and tried this and that scheme to make money—with pigs, with bees, with a kaffir store on his place—and sometimes Mary reluctantly tried to help; she especially hated serving native women in the kaffir store. They were dogged by bad luck. Charlie Slattery at first tried to give advice; he didn't want a run-down farm next to his own. Moreover, for a white farmer to sink below a decent level of prosperity was to let down the whole dominant white community. They wanted no "poor whites" around—British whites, of course. Charlie realized the case was hopeless when Dick had been weakened by several bouts of malaria and when Mary, after a vigorous effort to boss the working force of natives and to put the books in some sort of order—she had been a good secretary—sank into nervous exhaustion. Then Charlie took a hand and persuaded Dick to sell the place to him and to remain as a manager; but he was first to go "off the altitude" with his sick wife on a long vacation to the coast. This proposal brought on the catastrophe, which had been slowly and secretly building up. The marriage—in every way a mistake—had degenerated into that double solitude, which, observes Mrs. Lessing, any marriage, "even a bad one," becomes. That is, they were used to each other, even if they didn't communicate.

We know from the beginning what the catastrophe is to be. The novel opens with a newspaper item, labeled "Murder Mystery," reporting the murder of Mary Turner by the houseboy and his confession. "No motive has been discovered." And no motive, by a kind of instinctive conspiracy of silence in the district, is ever allowed to be discovered. Charlie Slattery and the sergeant of the local police force discourage, by their manner suggesting unvoiced threats, Marston, the young newly arrived English assistant who was to have taken over the management of the farm during Dick Turner's absence on the vacation Charlie had insisted upon and who, living for some weeks with the Turners, had been increasingly bewildered by the atmosphere of the household and by what he had seen of the relationship between Mary and the houseboy, Moses. Young Marston is asked by Charlie if he knows anything that would throw light on the murder, but when Marston fumbles in the effort to sort out impressions, Charlie immediately smells trouble. And the young man, ignorant of the country and its ways, cannot interpret what he has seen and is easily silenced. As for Dick Turner, the shock has sent him, weakened as he is, completely round the bend for good. And Moses, with a fatalism traditional in his tribal society where everyone knew what he could and could not do, accepted punishment and said nothing.

In this brilliant opening scene, which follows immediately upon the discovery of the murder, we see a civilization in action to protect itself. The district handles the Turner case with that "*esprit de corps* which is the first rule of South African society." The people do not ask questions. But young Marston, not yet assimilated, wondering how it all began, clings to the belief that there are causes that must be looked for a long way back, and that it is the causes that are important. Before he goes away, he asks himself the questions that are answered by the author: "What sort of woman had Mary Turner been, before she came to the farm and had been slowly driven off balance by heat and loneliness and poverty? And Dick Turner himself—what had he been? And the native—but here his thoughts were stopped by lack of knowledge. He could not even begin to imagine the mind of a native." Marston never even begins to imagine what part he himself had had in bringing on the end. Nor does he ever know. But we do. The author is omniscient.

After the opening scene, we are taken back to Mary's child-hood. Its background was the store, as it was for thousands up and down Southern Africa—the store near one of the many little railway stations, where the farmers came to get their mail, to read their letters from Home, to send off their grain to market, to buy their groceries, to drink and to gossip. But Mary didn't get driven there once a week—she lived within sight of it, for her father was a pumpman on the railway. It was the place she was always being sent to on errands by her mother and where she liked to linger, the place her mother hated be-cause her father bought his drink there, got into debt there. The family life of Mary until she was sixteen was something to forget, and her happiness when she escaped to her secretary's job in the town was something to look back upon from the miseries of the later years on the farm, something to dream of recovering when, after several years she ran away, only to find everything changed, and to let Dick take her back to the farm. The childhood memories return, in true Freudian fashion, to haunt the nightmares of her final breakdown and to throw a sinister light on her strange relationship with Moses.

The clear, detached, objective narrative moves ahead stead-ily, without experiments in technique or mannerisms of style; it builds up to dramatic scenes, then relaxes tension and con-tinues on a new course, determined by some new circumstance. Dick's first illness, for example, forces Mary to go out among the native farm workers and "boss the job"; a hopeful turn of affairs it seems at first, until the brutal episode of her irrational anger at the native Moses starts the train of events that ends in murder. The whip leaves a scar on the face of Moses. But he does not seem to nurse revenge and, when he replaces a dis-missed houseboy, he performs his duties quietly and efficiently. The hidden scar is on Mary's memory. Ironically, Moses' little acts of kindness when Mary is worn out with nursing Dick in his illness—little acts showing his concern for his mistress—transgress the unwritten laws concerning the relation of white and black in that particular society. Mary does not know what to do with any personal relation. If he tempts her to eat with something specially prepared on her tea-tray, or with a few flowers in a handleless cup, she is troubled by this desire to please her. She can not give the word of approval he is waiting for, but neither can she utter the rebuke called for, and she begins to feel somehow in his power. She desperately needs his help in the long weeks of Dick's slow convalescence and, after Dick is able to go out again to supervise the work, she is exhausted and sunk in apathy. Irrational fears and deep uneasiness take possession of her. "She was fighting against something she did not understand." Her dreams are obsessive nightmares. She tries to tell Dick to dismiss Moses, but she fears his anger at another evidence of her inability to get along with servants. "She felt as if she were in a dark tunnel, nearing something final, something she could not visualize, but which waited for her inexorably." Awaking from some nightmare, she would become aware of the noises from the bush—the movement of branches as if something heavy were pushing its way through them; "and [she] thought with fear of the low crouching trees all about."

We live so long with Mary in that tunnel—the little happenings of her waking hours scarcely less nightmarish than the dreams at night—that we forget how the drama playing itself out almost in secret in the little house would startle and dismay a spectator coming in suddenly almost at the end. Having brought Mary and Moses to the strange pass where they were like two antagonists, waiting, silently sparring, Mrs. Lessing invites us to take a look at the Turners from the outside. What is the gossip about them in the district? They themselves are totally ignorant of it. Charlie Slattery has been waiting for years for Dick to go bankrupt. He wants Dick's land for grazing, but Dick "sat tight on his debts and his farm." And at last Charlie goes over to see him. He inspects the farm with Dick, and then comes into the house, and a brilliantly detailed scene follows: a cruel picture of Mary, and a shocking revelation of the terms on which she is living with Moses. An expert in black-white behavior, in looks, tones of voice, ways of speech, Charlie goes white with anger at what takes place during the meal over which Mary tries to preside. He comes to the swift decision to buy the farm and to take Dick on as a mere assistant after Dick has taken Mary to the coast. He is ruthless in his expert handling of an intolerable situation. Dick has no strength to resist, though he has a real love of this farm of his. It begins to look as if the Turners could be rescued from the ultimate degradation. Young Marston is brought in to run the place in the absence of the Turners and to learn what is necessary before they go.

But there is Moses. A few days before they are to leave, Marston, who has spent all his time out on the land and who has slept in a little thatched hut, suffering from a touch of the sun, happens to stay near the house for the day. Coming to the house for some water, he sees the strange spectacle of Moses helping Mary button her dress, and then watching her brush her hair. Both Moses and Mary see him. Marston struggles through incomprehension to pity for Mary. Mary shifts from confused appeals to Marston for protection to resentment that he has come there—it was all right before he came. And her fears take over in her cry: "He won't go away." And then she suddenly orders Moses to go away. "Tony realized that she was trying to assert herself: she was using his presence there as a shield in a fight to get back a command she had lost." Moses says, quietly enough, "Madame wants me to go because of this boss?"

And Moses goes, into the bush. Mary waits through her last day with a sense of doom that she can do nothing to avert; a long day with some strange moments of self-realization, and others of seeing herself and her life as if from a great distance —Mary Turner as she had been, "that foolish girl travelling unknowingly to this end. . . ." The evil was there; but she did not know of what it consisted. "What had she done? Nothing, of her own volition. Step by step she had come to this, a woman without will, sitting on an old ruined sofa that smelled of dirt, waiting for the night to come that would finish her." Justly—she knew that. Oddly enough, Moses, who makes no attempt to escape after the midnight murder, also knows from his tribal inheritance the justice of retribution. That night "the trees advanced in a rush, like beasts, and the thunder was the noise of their coming." At the end, when Mary sees Moses moving out from the dark, she has an extraordinary feeling of guilt toward him, "to whom she had been disloyal." Is Doris Lessing here making her bitter comment on the civilization whose weaknesses are judged in this story of misfits and failures?

It is to be noted that Mrs. Lessing seems completely certain about Mary and amazingly mature in her psychological exploration. Equally to be remarked is her discretion in staying outside Moses, as it were; there is acute observation of his manner, his speech, his way of looking—everything that can be seen and heard. We see him with startling vividness. He waits, after his dreadful deed, for the lightning to illuminate for the last time the small house, the veranda, the huddled shape of Mary on the bricks—and with the flash comes "his final moment of triumph, a moment so perfect and complete that it took the urgency from thoughts of escape." He goes into the bush to wait for the pursuers who will come with the morning. Moses' emotion, if one likes, is guesswork. But Mrs. Lessing adds: "Though what thoughts of regret, or pity, or perhaps even wounded affection were compounded with the satisfaction of his completed revenge, it is impossible to say."

This first novel by Doris Lessing leaves an impression of controlled detachment, and I think most readers would be absorbed in the story without at any point identifying with Mary or Dick or Moses, unless a reader had one of those private connections with the experiences recorded that would influence his emotional response. One feels that everything—people, landscape, social order, and attitudes—has been closely observed and reflected upon, that there have been pity and indignation in the process, which make themselves felt in a bitter undercurrent of judgment on the conditions that make such tragic failures possible. There was, Mrs. Lessing told me, no particular crime like the murder of Mary Turner that she had knowledge of. There was gossip she sometimes heard, in the district she herself grew up in, about native servants being allowed to overstep the line of permissible relations between black houseboy and white mistress.

Detachment and understatement increase the horror of the book. But there is another feeling, which grows stronger towards the end, of a compulsive drive toward death and ruin. Perhaps, in accounting for this feeling, one may risk calling attention to a passage in *The Golden Notebook*. Anna, the novelist in that book, had written a first novel concerned with the color bar. So far as we are told anything about it, there is no resemblance at all to Mrs. Lessing's first novel, except for the theme. It is used as the basis for some very amusing scenes between Anna and scouts from television and cinema agencies looking for scripts. By the time they have outlined the changes that would have to be made in the novel, there is nothing left of the original story except the title. But these fruitless discussions turn Anna's mind back to the particular time and place—during the war and in Africa—when the idea of the novel came to her; and she realizes, looking back to those days, that it grew out of a nostalgia for death. She recalls the weekend at Mashopi, the hotel in the country outside of Salisbury, the moonlit scene, the smell of wet flower-beds, the sound of dance music, and her own feeling of a "dangerous delicious intoxication." This intoxication, as she knew even then, was "the recklessness of infinite possibility, of danger, the secret ugly frightening pulse of war itself, of the death we all wanted, for each other and for ourselves." (135) The emotion out of which the story shaped itself—a story that had nothing to do with what actually took place at Mashopi—was the "unhealthy, feverish excitement of wartime, a lying nostalgia, a longing for license, for freedom, for the jungle, for formlessness" The sequence of events she imagined was the externalization of the emotion, the objective correlative—as T. S. Eliot defined it in "Hamlet and His Problems," making the term popular some years ago among academic critics. "The root of that book was poisoned," reflects Anna. Anna's retrospective analysis throws a fascinating, if indirect light, on the atmosphere of *The Grass Is Singing* —prefixed, one remembers, by the quotation from *The Waste Land*—and on what critics term "objectivity."

II *Five*

After *The Grass Is Singing* the following works appeared in rapid succession: *This Was the Old Chief's Country*, ten short stories, all Rhodesian in theme and setting (1951); *Martha Quest* (1952), the first in a projected series of five novels; and in 1953 a group of five short novels or novelettes, *Five*, for which Doris Lessing won the Somerset Maugham Award in 1954 for the best work of fiction of the year by a writer under thirty-five. One story has an English setting; the background of the other four is Rhodesian. All show mastery of that form of fiction which Henry James called the *nouvelle* and which has been more successfully practiced in Continental Europe than in the United States and in England. It is roughly distinguished by the number of words—about 25,000 to 45,000; too long for a short story and too short for a novel, it is never very popular with publishers in England and in the United States. Ludwig Lewisohn years ago in *Expression in America* defined it with precision as a form having at its best the fine qualities of "isolation of material and depth of tone, restraint upon over-elaboration," yet with "the final effect of brimming fulness." Some themes, as all readers know, suffer from expansion, others from compression. The artist must have a sure instinct for what is right for a certain theme. Mrs. Lessing likes the *nouvelle*. In her preface to *African Stories*, she calls it a most enjoyable form, "although of course there is no way of getting them printed out of book form. There is space in them to take one's time, to think aloud, to follow, for a paragraph or two, on a side-trail—none of which is possible in a real short story."

Of the *Five, Hunger*, which she calls a failure, is "it seems, the most liked." When Mrs. Lessing was in Moscow with a delegation of writers in 1952, the British team, though its members differed among themselves politically, agreed that "writing had to be a product of the individual conscience or soul. Whereas the Russians did not agree at all" and there were many debates. The Russians were demanding in literature greater simplicity and simple judgments of right and wrong. The British argued against this. (Were they arguing for complexity and for shades of moral judgment?) But Mrs. Lessing recalls that while Dickens created all good and all bad characters, that didn't keep him from being a great writer; and she herself had Southern Africa behind her, "a society as startlingly unjust as Dickens's England. Why, then, could I not write a story of simple good and bad, with clear-cut choices, set in Africa? . . . Only one possible plot—that a poor black boy or girl should come from a village to the white man's rich town, and . . . there he would encounter, as occurs in life, good and bad, and after much trouble and many tears he would follow the path of. . . ." And

that is how *Hunger* came to be written. But she considered that
it failed and wasn't true.[1]

Hunger is a little too long, yet not long enough for a novel.
Mrs. Lessing attempts to do in this story of Jabavu, a native
youth right from the kraal and its tribal life, what she avoided
doing with Moses: somehow to make us share his experience,
feel what it would be like to be such a boy; to leave the tribal
life, hungry for what he had heard of the delights of the city; to
make the long journey on foot; to become the easy prey of both
white and black exploiters; but also to begin to make the difficult transition from the old way of life to a new one, with the
help of people who are working for a different and more hopeful future in a rapidly changing world. We have to know not
only what Jabavu does, what he seems like to the people, both
whites and blacks with whom he comes in contact, what they
do to him, but also how he feels and thinks, how he despairs
and hopes and exults, how and what he learns. He escapes
complete disaster, though at the worst moment he sinks into
the mindless fatalism that at the end possesses Moses. When
we leave Jabavu, however, it seems possible that he will eventually become one of the leaders of the new Africa.

There was danger that Jabavu's story might turn into an interesting case history, and read like a report by a thoroughly
competent sociologist. Mrs. Lessing rather likes case histories,
and some of her stories take on that aspect. But this one does
not. Jabavu comes to life—thanks to Mrs. Lessing's gift of conveying sensory impressions. We can test this in almost any
scene in *Hunger:* the native hut in which Jabavu and his
brother wake up at the beginning; or the shebeen in town
where Jabavu drinks that dreadful concoction called skokian—
and what a kick!—made of cornmeal, sugar, tobacco, methyl-
ated spirits, boot polish, and yeast.

Is the vicarious experience authentic? Who, of completely
different race and background, can say? Only some African,
perhaps, emerged from a Jabavu stage and become part of a
more advanced culture, might look back upon his primitive
past and say, "It was like that." It is worth considering how
Mrs. Lessing goes about trying to create the illusion of what it

is like to be Jabavu. She uses the present tense and a very simple, uncomplicated prose. The point of view, though, is that of the omniscient author, for gestures, acts, must be interpreted. Perhaps, as readers learn from the psychologists, the anthropologists, the sociologists, and the archeologists more of the strange ways of other cultures than their own, many explanations will become superfluous. And, too, the vividness of Mrs. Lessing's picturing is often self-explanatory and needs no comment. *Hunger* might well be more powerful if less expanded.

The author's imagination must go beyond what she may have seen and heard in the huts of some native compound when she opens her story with the awakening of Jabavu's family in the hut, or when she leads up to his determination to leave for the city. We enter the memory of Jabavu's mother—wondering about this strong-willed rebellious son, who survived the terrible year of the Long Hunger when she lost two others. But Jabavu was so demanding a child that the women used to laugh when they watched him suck: "That one was born hungry—that one will make a big man." When he is thinking of leaving, it does come into his head that his mother will die of grief. "Now he looks at his mother. He does not think of her as young, old, pretty, ugly. She is his mother, who came properly endowed to her husband, after a proper amount of cattle had been paid for her. She has borne five children, three of whom live. She is a good cook and respectful to her husband. She is a mother, as a mother should be, according to the old ideas. Jabavu does not despise these ideas: simply, they are not for him . . . Jabavu's wife will not be like his mother: he does not know why, but he knows it."

Out of the news that reaches the kraal from the city, Jabavu builds his dreams. But he is not just a dreamer. He teaches himself to read, after a fashion, from scraps of wrapping paper on packages bought from the Greek who keeps the store—comics, some of these papers are. The first word he learns is *Bang*, from the picture of the big white man on the white horse, firing a gun. Very puzzling, what the big white men do, rescuing the beautiful white girl, but beating up the little yellow men. He finds in the rubbish heap a child's alphabet. The process, made completely plausible, is also very funny; but it is also a great breeder of confusion in Jabavu's mind about the white man's world. Learning to read takes him months of sitting under a tree puzzling out words, while he acquires the reputation of being lazy. It is a triumph when he makes out his first sentence: "The African must eat beans and vegetables as well as meat and nuts to keep him healthy." He rolls on the ground with pride, laughing, saying, "That's what I shall eat when I go to white man's town." Sometimes, when he can make nothing of a sentence full of strange words, he walks miles to the next village to ask a man who knows English and who teaches him how to speak a good deal of it. He marks difficult words with charcoal on a newspaper, and saves the papers so that he can ask someone, sometime, their meaning. All this dreaming and learning goes on until he can go to the city when he is sixteen, hungry for life and for all the things the white men have; his head is full of distorted ideas, and he is obviously headed for trouble.

The device of a young man setting forth on a high road to unknown adventures is one of the oldest and most certain ways to capture the reader's attention. The interest in Jabavu's journey is fully sustained, and there are threats and promises in the incidents along the way. He proves himself quick-witted and clever in outwitting the lorry drivers engaged in tricking raw natives into going to the mines. Escaped from this trap, he makes up a little boasting song—a device Mrs. Lessing uses to excellent effect on several occasions. (It makes Jabavu akin to the boasters in *Beowulf*.)

> Here is Jabavu
> Here is the Big Mouth of the clever true words—
> I am coming to the city . . .
> I am Jabavu, who goes alone.

The most significant, for his future, of the adventures along the way, is his encounter one night with Mr. Samu, his wife, and her brother. Educated natives, they—as we immediately guess—go about awakening the untutored Africans to their true position. They have a brief case full of subversive literature. They feed Jabavu by their roadside fire, and are surprised to discover he can read; before long Mr. Samu is launched on a lecture, full of words strange to Jabavu: organization, politics, committees, trade unions. He explains how the white men have settled like locusts over Africa, and, like the locusts in early morning, cannot take flight because of the dew upon their wings; and "the dew that weights the white man is the money that he makes from our labor." (These locusts weighted with dew at sunrise are beautifully pictured in the short sketch "A Mild Attack of Locusts.") Jabavu is stunned by the strange new ideas; but he does grasp one thing: if he listens to these people and follows their plans, it will not mean the kind of life he wants—a bicycle, different food, a woman of the town (he has heard of them), dancing, music. He has also heard of these people who travel by night and have books not liked by the police. But he accepts a slip of paper from them, with a name and address in the town; and we know this will probably mean trouble for him. The struggle in Jabavu, beginning to take shape, is between what he wants for himself and what he is willing to give for others. Later, in the town, he learns from Mrs. Kambusi, who runs a combined brothel and liquor joint (shebeen) and who has a kind impulse to set Jabavu on the right road, that the people at the address are the "men of light."

So when Jabavu comes to the outskirts of the city, the slow narrative build-up, suitable for a short novel, has placed clearly before us not only Jabavu but the nature of the struggle he faces. We are prepared for his disillusionment, for his stealing (out of his complete ignorance), for his bursts of energy and pride, for his gullibility, for his suspicions. And we are also ready to accept the interest he arouses in good and bad people alike, who see promise in him for their own ends, whether good or evil. In the complications of a lively plot, there are echoes from a far shore: from the Artful Dodger, teaching little Oliver to steal—as the evil Jerry teaches Jabavu; from Mrs. Warren and her profession, bringing up her daughter to be respectable, as Mrs. Kambusi sends her children to the Catholic mission school; even from the murder of Nancy in *Oliver Twist* —though the motives of Jerry in stabbing Betty are different. And Jerry plots to introduce Jabavu into the house of Mr. Mizi, one of the men of light, to steal the money he thinks is hidden

there. The relationship that keeps Jerry and Jabavu tied together is itself a convincing psychological study.

The Africans in Jerry's group, who have been exposed to the
white civilization long enough to weaken the connection with
their tribal past, fail to understand the curious state of apathy
into which Jabavu falls after Jerry has cleverly stacked the
cards so that it seems Jabavu has stabbed Betty: "They do not
understand that what is happening in Jabavu is something very
old. His mind is darkening in despair, in accepting of what
destiny has willed for him, and is turning towards death. This
feeling of destiny, of fate, is very strong in the life of the tribe,
where guilt and responsibility for evil is decided by the old
ways of magic." And Jabavu has realized that, though he did
not kill Betty, he had wanted to be free of her. The white clergyman who reluctantly visits Jabavu in jail to bring him a letter
from Mr. Mizi, "the man of light," and to reassure him that his
jail sentence will not be long (the local police seem, by the
way, to be very efficient in getting the complicated story of the
murder and attempted robbery straight)—this clergyman is
familiar with the state of blank apathy into which natives sink
and is greatly surprised at the sudden flash of awakened life in
Jabavu when he reads the letter. The word that has meant most
to him in the long letter is *We*—"We greet you": "The life of
his fathers was built on the word *we*. Yet it was never for him.
And between then and now has been a harsh and ugly time
when there was only the word I, I, I—as cruel and sharp as a
knife . . . The word *we* has been offered to him again, accepting all his goodness and his badness, demanding everything he
can offer . . . and for the first time that hunger in him, which
has raged like a beast all his life, wells up, unrefused, and
streams gently into the word *We*."

A Home for the Highland Cattle is a story in a different
mood.

For Jabavu's mother a proper amount of cattle had been
paid by her husband—*lobola*, equivalent to a dowry. This story
turns upon the importance of cattle, even if the cattle are in a
picture. The scene is laid in the suburb of the town which we
have explored with Jabavu; but now we see it from the point of

view of the young English wife of a government civil servant who is newly arrived to work as soil expert for the Department of Lands Afforestation of the colony. Temporarily, until they can find a house of their own, they are occupying the furnished flat of a lady who is on holiday for several months. The flat is one in a long row of one-story boxes, with garden in front, connected yards in back, little sheds at the end of the yards for the house servants, and an alleyway behind them. The story is a comedy, and the stage set is important. The town has a population of some 10,000—actually about 150,000, but only the whites count; the blacks don't live there—they squeeze in as they can. The families of the servants stay in the native compounds, and that accounts for some interesting sex relations.

Marina, the young English wife, arrives with ideas almost as unrelated to actuality as were Jabavu's. She expects to find herself among a group of amiable people, "pleasantly interested in the arts, who read the *New Statesman* week by week, and held that discreditable phenomena like the colour bar and the black-white struggle could be solved by sufficient goodwill . . . a delightful picture." She soon learns about the efficacy of good-will when she tries to treat servants as she thinks they should be treated and arouses the hostility of her neighbors who have adjusted to native ways well enough to live on a working basis with the black-white situation and who do not want a new-comer upsetting the status quo. As for the Africans, they don't know what to make of their new mistress, but they do know enough to take advantage of her oddly generous behavior; and, when they are by themselves, out back in that yard, they have a lovely time mimicking her and their other employers. (Marina watches them with amazement and reluctant amusement through the half-drawn curtains of the kitchen.)

One of the furnishings of the flat is an eyesore to Marina, but a cherished heirloom to the absent owner—a mid-Victorian horror of Highland cattle, shaggy and ferocious creatures glaring down at her, from where they stand in sunset-tinted pools. The owner has given her special instructions to be careful of this picture. Marina wishes it would fall down and smash its frame, and is hopeful that the houseboy Charlie will do as much damage to it as he does to other objects. But he loves to look at it—such beautiful cattle! Charlie is an amiable and cheerful young man, in white shorts, a scarlet shirt, tartan socks, mauve suspenders, and white tennis shoes. Trouble develops when the next-door neighbor, Mr. Black, comes one night to complain to Marina about Charlie, who is singing lustily with his friends, out back in the shed. Marina's attitude infuriates Mr. Black—"I really fail to see why these people should not have a party." She suggests that there would be less noise if Mr. Black would turn down his own wireless. It is easy to see why Mr. Black becomes inarticulate and goes out to slug Charlie, but he hits his fist against Charlie's arm upraised to protect his head—and then calls the police. Marina attempts to get the record straight—"as a matter of accuracy, he [Charlie] did not hit you"—but in the eyes of the neighbors she is breaking the code and taking the side of the "niggers."

This scene is lively, funny, and very instructive to readers unfamiliar with this particular African colonial society. But the central episode arises out of Marina's response to a gay little scene she happens to observe from her kitchen window. Theresa, fifteen-year-old black nursemaid in Mr. Black's family, is hanging out the wash, and Charlie, at leisure, is courting her with dance and gesture. It is charming, but to Marina, recently come from a different culture, what is it but the seduction of a child? Theresa becomes pregnant, and no one worries except Marina. These things are all a part of the proper balance between white and black: "The balance was upset, not by Theresa, who played her allotted part, but by Marina, who insisted on introducing these Fabian scruples into a clear-cut situation." Mrs. Black has no intention of discharging Theresa, who continues to care for the Black children. But Marina feels that Charlie should marry Theresa. Marina's husband Philip, who is away much of the time on his duties, tries to enlighten her: Charlie has a wife in his distant kraal. If the families of the men who work in the town are not permitted—as they are not —to live there, prostitution is inevitable. "You talk about Theresa as if she were a vital statistic," says Marina. So she tries to arrange that Charlie accept Theresa as his town wife, so to say. Charlie is willing enough, provided Theresa's father, who lives in a "location" five miles away, can be persuaded. But where are the cattle for the *lobola?* The inspiration comes to Marina to present the Highland cattle to the old man—leaving, of course, a good sum behind in the furnished flat for the owner when she returns.

So they set out in Philip's car to see the old man. Charlie and Theresa are delighted with the joy ride in a white man's car, the Highland cattle balanced precariously on Charlie's knee. Marina has never seen the "location," and the sight fills her with the most acute indignation. We are made to see it, too. When, leaving the car, they walk through a dreary waste land, Marina has subsided into a mood of grim despair. The old man's shack is made of sheets of corrugated iron, bound at the corners with string, with big stones keeping the roof from flying away in the wind. The old man is at first definitely hostile to this bargain, and accepts it only after a long reproachful speech in which he contrasts the old and the new ways, telling how he had wooed Theresa's mother, with gifts and courtesies between the clans, and how the ten great cattle had been chosen and driven over to Theresa's family. He thus reminds the two young people and himself of the time when every action had its ritual, when the cattle were not to be thought of in terms of a bargain, but in those of a symbol. They meant good feeling, "a token of union between the clans, an earnest that the woman would be looked after, an acknowledgment that she was something very precious." Concluding his speech, he spits contemptuously on the ground, lifts the picture, takes it into the dark hut, looks at it, seems pleased in a way, but soon draws a blanket over his head, and squats down inside the door.

Up to this point in the story, the picture has seemed ridiculous, but now it has taken on the meaning of an old way of tribal life that had had its dignity. And this pathetic scene recalls the note struck at the beginning of the story. In a brief description of the town and its history, the almost legendary figure of the chief Lobengula is recalled. Under the Big Tree in his kraal used to sit "the betrayed, sorrowful, magnificent King in his rolls of black fat and beads and gauds, watching his doom approach in the white people's advance from the south, and dispensing life and death according to known and honored customs." A sense of the African past, in some concrete image, is seldom absent from Mrs. Lessing's Rhodesian stories; its presence enriches their pattern.

The term of their occupancy of Mrs. Skinner's flat comes to an end, Marina and Philip find themselves a house in one of the new suburbs, and Mrs. Skinner comes back to find the Highland cattle gone. She doesn't believe Charlie's story, and is not placated by the generous eight pounds left to pay for the picture. Since other little odds and ends are missing, she calls the police. Charlie with other handcuffed Africans, all quite cheerful—they usually prefer a fortnight's free board and lodging in jail to a fine—is on his way to jail when Marina, turning into a shop, notices the now-familiar sight of a file of handcuffed blacks passing, their women straggling after them. For a moment she thinks one of them looks like Charlie, but she remembers he was supposed to go on a visit to his village, and she dismisses the thought. By this time she is becoming adjusted to seeing vital statistics rather than individual human beings.

Jabavu, Marina, and the Turners do not look at the African landscape. But in *Eldorado* Alec Barnes, who came from England with his Scotch wife to find a farm and to grow food—not to make money on tobacco or to look for gold—used to stand at the edge of a field, gazing across at a ridge of bush which "rose sharp to the great blue sky; or at the edge of the big vlei, which cut across the farm in a shallow, golden swathe of rustling grasses, with a sluggish watercourse showing green down its centre. He would stand on a moonlight night staring across the fields which now appeared like a diffusing green sea, the white crests of the maize shifting like foam; or at midday, looking over the stretching acres of brown and heaving clods, warm and rich with sunlight; or at sunset, when the miles of bush flared gold and red. Distance—that was what he needed. It was what he had left England to find." Alec had been a clerk in a bank, like Doris Lessing's father, and, like him, was a dreamer. He found space, but he was not a good farmer, for he disregarded the advice of experts—and what that was, and why, we learn; and this kind of knowledge makes Mrs. Lessing's Africa live for us. Hundreds of miles south of the rich pocket of earth where his farm was located were the gold-bearing reefs of Johannesburg; hundreds of miles north were the rich copper mines—the "two lodestars of the great central plateau"—and all around the rich pocket of soil were the wastes of the light sandveld, good for tobacco.

This is in a way a success story—an ironic success, not at all what Alec wanted, or what his wife wanted. Maggie, his wife, approves of growing food—it fits in with the ideas of her religious, farming grandparents; and she hates the idea of "luck," of "gambling." Alec's love of space and distance is fatal to his farming because it leads him to clear more and more land, although his farm needs small fields with trees to guard them from winds and girdles of grass to hold the soil against the flooding rains. So the farm never promises more than a scanty living. Their one son Paul grows up, adventurous and strong, and Maggie pins her hopes on him, on his going away to school and winning scholarships, but Alec will have to make the farm pay, if any such future is to be assured for Paul. Part of the story is the long-drawn-out contest over Paul, with Paul himself pulled first in one direction and then in the other. He goes away to school, but each time he returns during holidays, he finds the atmosphere more and more disturbing, his father more and more given over to dreams, his mother more and more unhappy.

With the cutting down of the trees, Alec can look into the distance to the ridge boundary, where there is a small gold mine, owned by a man who has lived there for years, working a small but steady seam. This old miner, Charlie, sometimes drops in of an evening; Alec, contemptuous at first of this little mine, begins to be fascinated by a dream of gold. Paul, during one holiday, visits the mine, and he and Charlie become friends. Then one night an old weatherbeaten prospector—one of a vanishing race—passing through, stays at the farm. "The old man spoke of the search for gold as a scientist might of discovery, or an artist of his art." Alec's new dream involves study of the soil, buying of geological maps and gold-panning equipment, and the use of a metal divining rod to discover gold, just as a hazel rod discovers water.

Maggie, now begininng to feel helpless about Alec, first listlessly, then with increasing interest, studies the maps, reads the books, gains some intimation of the wonderful future of this continent; and she shifts her hopes for Paul. Perhaps he could become a scientist, an engineer. Alec's lunacy she even accepts: "There must always be a moment when the practical-minded must pay tribute to it"—this "visionary moon-chasing quality." Both Maggie and Paul—reluctantly, contemptuously, through various moods—are drawn into Alec's lunacy. The old miner, Charlie James, becomes a kind of surrogate father to Paul. He takes him into partnership; and using perfectly sober and tried ways, they do discover a fairly hopeful seam in the old mine. Maggie is afraid that Alec will be very bitter at his own defeat, but the old dreamer is pleased—"I always said there was gold there." And he is happy to be allowed to go tapping around with his diving rod. Maggie has been defeated, for the lure of "luck," of something for nothing, has won her son. She has clung to her Scotch belief that "knoweldge frees a man"—and grieves all her life because that simple and obvious truth was not obvious to Paul.

The novelette form has been ample enough to do full justice to each of the characters, to the shifting attitudes and emotions over a period of time, to the attraction of Africa, with its magnets—gold, copper, tobacco—that "drew men, white and black; drew money from the world's counting-houses."

The Antheap is about a gold mine in a great hollow in the mountains, approached through a pass among sharp peaks; hot and close and dry half the year, warm and steamy during the rains. Gold had been sought there through the centuries, back to the Bushmen; hundreds of years ago, Arabs came from the coast with slaves and warriors, looking for gold for the Queen of Sheba. At least "no one has proved they did not." At the turn of the twentieth century a big mining company had set up machinery, sunk shafts, and then left to seek a place where the reefs lay more evenly. Then the Scotsman, Macintosh, who had made one fortune and lost it in Australia, and made another in New Zealand, which he still had, bought the rights. "He simply hired hundreds of African laborers and set them to shovel up the soil in the centre of that high, enclosed hollow in the mountains, so that there was soon a deeper hollow, then a vast pit . . . then a gulf like an inverted mountain. Mr. Macintosh was taking great swallows of the earth, like a gold-eating monster, with no fancy ideas about digging shafts or spending money on roofing tunnels." A lively description of the mining process explains why the Africans called it the "pit of death" and named Mr. Macintosh the "Gold Stomach," but they came in their hundreds to work there. Mr. Macintosh employed only one white man, his engineer, Mr. Clarke; he kept his own books; he paid six boss boys very well and treated them like important people. He was far away from any active interference by the law. He was one of the richest men in the country, altogether a fine example of an old-timer in that tough world.

Mr. Clarke, the engineer, was glad of the security of his job, and so was Mrs. Clarke; and, as their small son Tommy grew older, and Mr. Macintosh took a liking to him, Mrs. Clarke knew that would mean something for Tommy's future. In fact Mrs. Clarke in her matter-of-fact way liked and admired Mr. Macintosh, and he liked her direct way of getting what she needed from him. Mr. and Mrs. Clarke lived amiably together. It was, however, a very silent household—no conversation, no explanations. There on one side of the great gulf of the mine were the two houses of the four white people, and on the other side, completely separated, was the native compound where the African workers and their families lived. The silence of Tommy's home led him, when he was old enough to go about alone, to escape to the friendly din of the compound to play with the "dirty kaffirs." And so he came to know a boy of his own age, Dirk; and the story is that of their difficult friendship, and what it did for them both, and how Mr. Macintosh became involved against his will and was eventually defeated and found himself doing things that went quite against the grain.

The silence of Tommy's home was in contrast to all the never-ceasing noises of the mine. The mine-stamps thudding gold, gold, never stopping; the picks ringing on stone, the clang of trucks, the roar of falling earth, the rumbling of trolleys on rails, the shouting and singing of the workers; and at night the hooting of owls and screaming of night-jars; and the rolling of thunder among the peaks—it was never silent except that once the machinery stopped, and that terrified the little boy—"as if the heart of the world had gone silent." He lay in bed at night, listening to the thud of the stamps; and in the compound, where they were singing and dancing around the fires, the drums beat against the thud of the stamps, and the dancers yelled—"a high undulating sound like a big wind coming fast and crooked through a gap in the mountains."

After a bad attack of malaria, Tommy is ordered to stop playing with the dirty kaffirs and is thus thrown back upon himself. Then he spends hours lying on the edge of the pit, looking down at the men far below, working like ants, climbing up the sides on steps cut in the earth and on flimsy ladders. It was like an enormous ant-working: "Heaps of the inert, heavy yellow soil, brought up from the bottom, lay all around him." Idly, at first, he begins to handle it. And so Tommy takes the first steps to becoming an artist. Deprived of his playmates in the compound, experiencing loneliness, he forms the yellow clay into little figures, calling them Betty and Freddy and Dirk. It is Dirk who risks coming to the back door with a new-born tiny duiker—a little buck—as a present. It dies—but Tommy begins to wonder and to ask questions about Dirk: why is he yellow and not dark brown? "They come in different colors," says his taciturn father. "He's a half-caste," says his mother. It is not long before the very observant Tommy, realizing there are only two white men at the mine, knows that Mr. Macintosh must be Dirk's father; and he has noticed how Dirk laughs, and how Mr. Macintosh laughs.

Mrs. Lessing has made a fascinating and convincing story of these two boys, and the growth over several years of their friendship in the face of obstacles, both outside and within them. Boys outwitting older people who are set against their deepest desires provide one of those universal stories we all want to hear. And this one of Dirk and Tommy, with its own very special circumstances in the African social and racial system, is convincing on all levels. That little private retreat or hide-out dear to children is for Dirk and Tommy a little hut in the bush where no one goes, which grows with their growing skill into a nice little shelter with shelves where Tommy puts his clay figures and the books he brings back from school on his vacations so that he can teach Dirk. On one vacation he returns to find no Dirk to greet him; Mr. Macintosh has put the eleven-year-old boy to work in the mine. Mrs. Clarke intervenes: "Tommy's upset—he's been used to Dirk and now he's got no one to play with." Earlier he had startled and alarmed his mother by asking—"Why shouldn't I play with Mr. Macintosh's son?" Later Dirk himself refuses to work in the mine even when Tommy is at school, quoting a law about age limits—as if Mr. Macintosh cared about laws. But Macintosh is no match for Tommy because the aging man loves him and so is vulnerable, and Tommy learns by instinct and experiment how to get what he wants. Mr. Macintosh makes various offers to Tommy's parents to put him on the road to a career—in the Merchant Navy, for one thing; but Tommy sulkily resists—why do they want always to make something of me? he demands of Dirk. Dirk, for his part, knows just what he wants—to be an engineer. Asked if he wants to go to college, Tommy inquires: "Why do you want to send me to college?" And Mr. Macintosh falls into the trap. "I have no children," he says sentimentally. "I feel for you like my own son." Tommy merely looks away toward the compound.

Tommy educates Dirk in more ways than one; by books, yes. But also by reports of how people live in the city—even the words to describe that life represent things completely unknown to the African. Tommy knows there is a school in the city for Colored—the half-caste and other non-African but colored races. Dirk could go there. But—and here is a neat little trick of racial injustice—Dirk knows that, if he did go to such a school, he could not see his black mother again. If he lives with the natives, he can't go with the half-castes, and vice versa. Tommy has never seen Dirk's mother—Macintosh's mistress. He asks Dirk to take him to see her. She is a gentle woman; and, besides Dirk, she has a bronze girl, a little black girl, and an almost white baby. Tommy, obscurely moved to expression in one of the mediums he now works with at odd moments— sometimes it is clay and sometimes soft wood—chooses carefully a piece of wood, and fights with it for many days with a new and unwieldy tool, fashioned out of a piece of metal from a scrap heap. He makes a statue of Dirk's mother, her arms lifted to the weight of a baby; but the face is blank—he has had no time to finish it before returning to school. He also fashions a bronze little girl, using boot polish to color the wood.

The contest goes on, but Mr. Macintosh begins to be dangerously ill-tempered, partly because he also is bewildered to find himself balked in what he wants—something he is quite unused to. And Tommy turns sulky and brings home bad marks; only in wretched little courses in art, in current events, and in the laws of Africa does he show any interest. In anything relating to the color question he not only reads up on his own, but he transmits the knowledge to Dirk, who in his turn begins to teach some of the young men in the compound. And one night Macintosh, coming home from the "other hut" where his mistress is, sees a light in Dirk's hut, where Dirk and half a dozen other boys are reading a newspaper. Macintosh is after all a Scot—here is education going on—Dirk is half a Scot, a chip off the old block, even if a chip of the wrong color. He begins to think Dirk could be used to teach his overseers. But there is nothing easy in the working out of this complicated study of human relations and tangled emotions. Tensions build up to a dramatic scene in which Macintosh comes to the boys' hut in their absence and sees some of Tommy's figures of clay and wood. "There was Dirk's mother, peering at him in bashful sensuality from over the baby's head, there the little girl, his daughter, squatting on spindly legs and staring. And there, on the edge of the shelf, a small, worn shape of clay which still held the vigorous strength of Dirk." As he stepped back to see these statuettes more clearly, still holding back his anger, he slipped on a piece of wood, "and there was the picture Tommy had carved and colored of his mine. Mr. Macintosh saw the great pit, the black little figures tumbling and sprawling over into the flames, and he saw himself, stick in hand, astride on his two legs at the edge of the pit, his hat on the back of his head." To him it seemed a monstrous injustice that Tommy thought of him thus.

But Mr. Macintosh is a man who works things out, capable of generosities of feeling and action. And he acts. The laddies win. Dirk is to go to a school where he can learn to be an engineer, Tommy to a university, perhaps eventually to an art school. He has discovered that art is a weapon, not just a sort of game to be played. How he has discovered it has been by watching Macintosh's face while he worked on a statue of Dirk. Though the boys have fought together and hated and resented each other, and felt themselves held together against their will, yet the friendship has endured.

"Why didn't you come near me all this time?" Tommy asked.

"I get sick of you," said Dirk. "I sometimes feel I don't want to see a white face again, not ever. I feel that I hate you all, every one."

"I know," said Tommy . . . And the last strain of dislike between them vanished.

Mrs. Lessing is not given to indulgence in symbols. But the statue Tommy carves out of a big fanged root, while Macintosh looks on, can scarcely be anything else. Macintosh hates it; Dirk, who is the subject of the statue, hates it. Neither knows what art is, but they are disturbed by it. "Slowly, the big fanged root which rose from the trunk was taking Dirk's shape." Macintosh, uneasily watching, says the ants will probably eat it or the veld fire will burn it. But to Tommy only the making of it matters—an attitude totally foreign to Mr. Macintosh's "accumulating nature." As the days pass and Macintosh watches, it is with increasing fear and dislike:

Dirk's long, powerful body came writhing out of the wood like something struggling free. The head was clenched back, in the agony of the birth, eyes narrowed and desperate, the mouth—Mr. Macintosh's mouth—tightened in obstinate purpose. The shoulders were free, but the hands were held; they could not pull themselves out of the dense wood, they were imprisoned. His body was free to the knees, but below them the human limbs were uncreated, the natural shapes of the wood swelled to the perfect muscled knees. . . . (*African Stories*, 375-76)

I have a notion Mrs. Lessing likes Mr. Macintosh. A Mr. Mc-Farline, also an elderly Scotsman, figures briefly in the adolescence of Martha Quest—a man quite in character: "A charming wicked old Scotsman who lived alone on his mine, which he worked in a way which cost him the very minimum in money, but a good deal in human life. There were always accidents on his mine. Also his native compound was full of half-caste children, his own. He was extremely wealthy and very popular. He gave generously to charity; and was about to stand for Parliament for one of the town constituencies." He drove young Martha to town, not quite sure whether to treat her as a budding maiden or a child to be given a present of a ten shilling note. "If I refuse it," thought Martha, "he will think it is because of the way he tried to touch me." So she took it and thanked him politely. (*Martha Quest*, 49-50) It is in Mr. McFarline's gold-eating pit that the prehistoric monster is imprisoned, alive, in Martha Quest's dream.

CHAPTER 3

The Short Stories

I *African Themes, African Landscape*

DORIS LESSING has published over fifty short stories, collected in four volumes.[1] Some of them first appeared in magazines in England and in the United States. The latest volume, *African Stories*, includes the ten that were published in *This Was the Old Chief's Country* (1951), two rescued from magazines, and two very early stories hitherto unpublished. *The Habit of Loving* (1957), out of seventeen stories, contains none with African settings and *A Man and Two Women* (1963), only two, but these two are among the very best of the African group. They belong with earlier stories that draw upon memories of growing up on the Rhodesian farm, and are sometimes written in the first person and appear to be directly autobiographical. But sometimes they are in the third person, with an observer who is often a young girl, or one who lived in the district and is recalling local gossip about people and happenings that aroused speculation.

All these African stories create in the reader's imagination a total impression of an African landscape—south-central geographically—a landscape with figures and an immense overarching sky. The figures are natives; white farmers of both British and Afrikaans (Boer) extraction and their families; odd characters like Leopard George; lonely women on isolated farms; and crowds of neighbors at week-end parties. And not only human figures. Because of the vivid descriptions of insect and animal life, the reader carries away nightmarish visions of ants, destroying abandoned homes, stripping the bones of dead or dying animals, eating out galleries in mud walls. Add leopards, crocodiles, beautiful young bucks, silhouetted against the horizon, and locusts, after their destructive raid on the maize, fanning their wings at sunrise to free them of the night dew. "It

looked as if every tree, every bush, all the earth were lit with
pale flames."

Mrs. Lessing conveys the beauty of the landscape as naturally as she writes. But there is another impression, too, and that
is fear. The young girl walking alone over the veld on a silent
hot morning feels a chill creeping up from the small of her back
to her shoulders, a tingling sensation at the roots of her hair,
and she realizes that this is the fear she has heard about but
never before experienced:

I had read of this feeling, how the bigness and silence of Africa, under the ancient sun, grows dense and takes shape in the mind, till
even the birds seem to call menacingly, and a deadly spirit comes
out of the trees and the rocks. You move warily, as if your very passing disturbs something old and evil, something dark and big and
angry that might suddenly rear and strike from behind. You look at
groves of entwined trees, and picture the animals that might be
lurking there; you look at the river, running slowly, dropping from
level to level through the vlei, spreading into pools where at night
the buck comes to drink, and the crocodiles rise and drag them by
their soft noses into underwater caves.

A meaningless terror and panic grip her for what seem hours,
but are only minutes. "This was the sort of fear that contracts
the flesh of a dog at night and sets him howling at the full
moon." (*The Old Chief Mshlanga*)

This fear is never made the dominant theme of a story, but it
recurs as a minor note often enough with different people to
make it a significant part of our impression of Africa. George,
known in his later years, for good reason, as Leopard George,
had never felt fear until he went out in search of the leopard
which had killed his mistress. "He was gazing at a towering
tumbling heap of boulders that stood sharp and black against a
high fresh blue, the young blue of an African morning, and it
was as if that familiar and loved shape moved back from him,
reared menacingly like an animal and admitted danger—a
sharp danger, capable of striking from a dark place that was a
place of fear."

Mrs. Gale, going out alone in the moonlight to inspect the
cabin where the new assistant was to live, did so with reluc-

tance, not liking to go outside her garden at night. She did not know what made her afraid, certainly not the natives who were merely pathetic children to her. She moved out along the glimmering white road, bordered by the black shadows of sparse stumpy trees, deliberately slowing her steps as a discipline, "moving through the pits of shadow, gaining each stretch of moonlight with relief." (*The De Wets Come to Kloof Grange*)

The autobiographical "Story of Two Dogs" recreates a child's world, with grown-ups on the outer fringes. Jock was the brother's dog; when his master was away at school, he became the mother's pet invalid, for she had a pathetic need for something delicate to nurse and protect, and he filled the role, to the great relief of father and both children. Had they allowed themselves to be delicate, "there would have been no need for Jock to sit between my mother's knees, his loyal noble head on her lap, while she caressed and yearned and suffered." It was decided that Jock must have someone to play with; otherwise, like Tommy in *The Antheap,* he would go off to play in the native compound with "those dirty Kaffir dogs," miserable beasts kept hungry so that they would hunt fresh meat for their masters. Jock would slink back from truancy in the compound to gaze soulfully into his mistress's eyes.

On one of the family treks to pay a round of visits, a mad little puppy was found to be a companion to Jock and to be the little girl's own pet. When they arrived at this neighbor's farm, the puppy hurled itself at the car, yapping deliriously; its owner said it had been stark staring mad with the moon every night for a week. It was just this wildness that appealed to the romantic little girl, because the story was that the puppy had a bandit father—an outlaw. During the holidays brother and sister tried, without much success, to train both dogs by jolly outdoor excursions through the bush and out on the veld. The long walks and the half-hearted hunting brought them rewards like hunting with a camera; they watched duikers at sunrise, outlined against the sky in warm gold, then dancing on the edge of the green bush where the children lay hidden. The dogs developed their own games and in time became almost wild, especially Bill with the outlaw blood, who corrupted Jock. They became even more independent when both children were away at school, and their mother wrote that the dogs treated the house like a hotel, returning for a meal or a day's sleep. It all ended rather sadly, as indeed it had to, what with the dogs reverting to egg-stealing and being injured by the traps to catch game set in the bush by the natives.

A young girl in "The Sun between Their Feet" spends a long hot African day in a deserted sandy spot, watching beetles trying to roll a ball of dung up a steep slope, as if they were conquering Mt. Everest. She lies low on the ground to see their project with their eyes, and she recalls what she has read in books about insects and their marvelous instincts. Close observation of the beetles leads her to conclude that they are very stupid. Interested in symbols, a reviewer singled this story out as the key story in the collection, *A Man and Two Women*, because the frustrated beetles suggested to him the general frustration in Doris Lessing's world; however, the little girl was certainly not frustrated, but enlightened.

The Golden Notebook several times uses a pushing-boulders-up-a-mountain image that suggests something beyond frustration: a great black mountain represents human stupidity; a group of people push a boulder up the mountain; when they have got a few feet up, there is a war or the wrong sort of revolution, and the boulder rolls down, but always ends a few inches higher than when it started, and the people start pushing again; a few great men stand at the top of the mountain and sometimes look down to see if the boulder-pushers are still on duty; but meanwhile they are meditating about the nature of space, or "what it will be like when the world is full of people who don't hate and fear and murder."

The fifteen-year-old boy in "Sunrise on the Veld" is given an insight into the ways of nature that shocks him and forces upon him questions that he will have to think about. Joy and physical well-being, as he runs and leaps along the path through the bush on a lovely morning before sunrise, fill him until he almost reaches the ecstasy of the glory and freshness of the Wordsworthian dream. "He felt his life ahead of him as a great and wonderful thing." He began to sing, and the sound echoed down the river gorge. Then he heard a new voice in the morning chorus of sounds—a strange scream. A small buck, disabled by a broken leg and caught in the bush, was being eaten by swarms of great black ants, flowing like "glistening black water through the grass." This is pretty horrible even to read about. The boy felt in his own limbs "the myriad swarming pain of the twitching animal." He was overwhelmed, as he watched, by the knowledge of fatality, of what has to be, of how life goes on, "by living things dying in anguish." He thought how, an hour ago, this small creature had been stepping proud and free through the bush, as he himself had done. Perhaps some native had thrown a stone—as he had often done at some creature like this; with the grim stoicism of realizing that things are like this on the vast, unalterable cruel veld, came also a sense of responsibility. "He saw himself, on any one of these bright ringing mornings, drunk with excitement, taking a snapshot at some half-seen buck"—and then not bothering to see even if he had missed or not. The death of that small animal was a thing that concerned him—"it lay at the back of his mind uncomfortably" —as he turned to go home to breakfast, leaving the trickles of ants disappearing into the dust. "The whispering noise was faint and dry, like the rustling of a cast snakeskin."

The young girl can be as absorbed in observing the ways of grown-ups as in watching the beetles. In several of the stories —among them "Getting Off the Altitude" and "Old John's Place"—Kate, thirteen or so, is with her parents at a week-end party held at one of the farmhouses in the district. She is too young to be left behind and too old to be parked with the numerous babies and little children in bedrooms and nurseries. The embarrassment of not belonging anywhere is beautifully realized. But the embarrassment is not hers alone; drifting about, she overhears scraps of conversation she is not supposed to hear, or comes upon couples in sheltered spots on the veranda, or in the pantry. For on these occasions there is an attitude of tolerance about relationships between the sexes—and Kate becomes aware of all sorts of puzzling problems. At the outset the sexes are segregated. There is always a stage in the party when the women sit at one end of the veranda and the men at the other, and the hostess, growing desperate in her attempts to get the party going, goes from one group to the other.

> Between the two separate groups wandered a miserable child, who was too old to be put to bed with the infants, and too young to join the party; unable to read because that was considered rude; unable to do anything but loiter on the edge of each group in turn, until an impatient look warned her that something was being suppressed for her benefit that would otherwise add to the gaiety of the occasion. As the evening advanced and the liquor fell in the bottles, these looks became more frequent.

The chief theme of "Old John's Place" is the temporary intrusion into the settled life of the district of the type of resident who buys a farm, "settling on it with a vagabond excitement," and flying off after a year or two, "leaving behind them a sense of puzzled failure." The reason usually given was that the wife was not cut out for farm life. The character sketches of the Sinclairs and the Laceys are held together by the fact that they were successive buyers of Old John's Place, a farm unlucky for some reason and therefore always changing hands. Both Mrs. Sinclair and Mrs. Lacey tried their best in very different ways to raise the tone of the district society, and both of them fascinated and puzzled Kate, enlarged her vision of the complexities of human relations, and gave her confused intimations of the mysteries of love and the nature of corruption. The social life of the district, the moral codes, the cultural level, are all admirably seen through the eyes of a growing girl, and they are pointed up by the contrast between the settled farmers of the district and the birds of passage.

Then there are the Slatters in "Getting Off the Altitude." Mr. Slatter is a tough, brutal, successful farmer, whose affair with a distant neighbor is a matter of common gossip. Mrs. Slatter, married all these years—their sons are almost grown—to a man who, she says apologetically, "doesn't know his own strength," has reached a point when literally and figuratively she needs to "get off the altitude." Living at a height of three to four thousand feet for years, people show the strain and need a vacation at sea level. Kate sometimes stays with the Slatters on occasions like big parties and, wandering around the rooms, she sometimes sees Mrs. Slatter when she is off guard and unaware of being observed. Kate, precociously acute, sees farther than she should into the sexual and emotional problems of the pathetic middle-aged woman, whom, she observes, her own father likes. Kate, had she kept on learning about the grown-ups at parties, would have qualified for the role of Henry James's Maisie.

Where are the natives in these African short stories? Usually in the background, serving the whites, although they sometimes play leading parts. There is the Old Chief Mshlanga, to whom all the land near the girl's farm had once belonged, whom she met several times on a path traversed by natives moving over the country, and once exchanged greetings with, and from whom she learned a lesson in courtesy quite at odds with the training she had received in black-white relations. She even walked miles to the kraal where he and a few others of his tribe still lived. This is a very significant little story, telling much in very few words. Since the narrative shifts to the first person, it is reasonable to regard it as a stage in Doris Lessing's own awakening to the Color problem.

It was quite unheard of that a young white girl should be walking the veld alone and "in this part of the bush where only Government officials had the right to move." And at her coming to the kraal everybody was embarrassed: the old men, the brightly clad chattering women, the chief himself, leaning against a tree, with a dozen old men sitting cross-legged around him. It was a village of ancients and children and women. All the young men were away working on white men's farms and mines, except for two or three temporarily on holiday, acting as the chief's attendants. The girl had come out of curiosity, because the cookboy on her father's farm was said to be the Old Chief's son. She did not know what to reply to the reserved greeting of the Old Chief. The village of thatched huts, "lovingly decorated with patterns of yellow and red and ochre mud on the walls," with its neat patches of mealies and pumpkins and millet, its cattle grazing under trees, its hens and goats, was altogether different from the dirty and neglected farm compound, the temporary, rootless home for migrant workers. "I walked away from the indifferent village, over the rise past the staring amber-eyed goats, down through the tall stately trees into the great rich valley where the river meandered and the pigeons cooed tales of plenty and the woodpecker tapped softly." And she felt a queer hostility in the landscape that seemed to say "you walk here as a destroyer. . . . I had learned that if one cannot call a country to heel like a dog, neither can one dismiss the past with a smile in an easy gush of feeling, saying: I could not help it, I am also a victim."

A sharper lesson came not long afterwards when goats belonging to the Old Chief trespassed on her father's crops and did damage that could be paid for only by confiscating the goats. That meant the Old Chief's people would go hungry when the dry season came. "Go to the police, then," said my father. The cookboy translated the Old Chief's parting words: "All this land, this land that you call yours, is his land, and belongs to our people." The upshot was the discovery that only through some oversight had the kraal not been removed long ago, and the oversight was soon remedied. The Old Chief and his people were transferred from this fertile valley to a native reserve hundreds of miles away, and the land was opened to white settlement. A year later the girl visited the village again. "Mounds of red mud, where the huts had been, had long swathes of rotting thatch over them, veined with the red galleries of the white ants . . . The pumpkin vines rioted everywhere. . . ."

"Leopard George" creates another picture of the past, when a kind of feudal relationship, kindly in its way, had sometimes been possible between a "good" master and his servants. Lucky, later Leopard, George, son of an old settler with a good name among the natives of the district, returns a hero from World War I, buys himself a wild tract of land, develops it, builds a substantial house, and finds all this possible because Old Smoke—once his father's servant—brings a fine gang of his own kinsmen to work on the farm, with his nephew to boss them. He also provides a young girl, his daughter, to be George's mistress. At one of George's parties she so far oversteps the color line as to come boldly to the edge of the group. So George sends her away, providing for her at a mission school; and he then takes on another girl, one who appears promptly and whom he does not know, at first, to be the newest young wife of Old Smoke. He does not allow her so many privileges as her predecessor; in fact, he makes her go back after her nightly visit, through the bush to her compound. She is terrified at this mile-long walk—and rightly so, for she disappears, and it is only too clear what has happened to her. George's pursuit and killing of the leopard form a stirring narrative. After this episode he changes all his habits; the week ends are hunting expeditions; he earns his nickname. But the friendly relationship with Old Smoke and his tribe is at an end. The episode is exciting enough, but the achievement of the story is the full-length portrait of Leopard George.

"The Nuisance" opens with a charming vignette of native women at the well near their compound—a well that in the dry season has to be used also by the farm. It ends grimly enough with what was fished out of the well: what remained of "the nuisance." She was the cross-eyed, hideous, floppy-breasted first wife of "the Long One," who was an artist in handling the cattle on the farm, with a "delicate brutality." It was like watching a circus act to see how he managed a team of sixteen fat, tamed oxen. "Alongside the double line of ponderous cattle that strained across acres of heavy clods, danced, raved, and screamed the Long One, with his twelve-foot-long lash circling in black patterns over their backs." But there was never a mark on them. The farmer used to say, "He knows how to handle oxen, but he can't handle his women." And eventually Long One's troubles with his three wives began to interfere with his work—troubles he came to discuss, man to man, with the farmer. He was terribly attractive to women. "I have seen him slouch down the road . . . his whip trailing behind in the dust, his trousers sagging in folds from hip-bone to ankle, his eyes broodingly directed in front of him, merely nodding as he passed a group of women among whom might be his wives. And it was as if he had lashed them with his whip. They would bridle and writhe; and then call provocatively after him. . . ."

The Long One's incessant complaints finally drove the farmer to tell him to hold his tongue and manage his women himself. And he did. The old wife disappeared; he said she had gone away; and everything was peaceful, until the time came when the old well had to be used. The rest of this very vivid story can be guessed. Perhaps the Nuisance killed herself—or slipped and fell. "Later we talked about the thing, saying how odd it was that natives should commit suicide; it seemed almost like an impertinence, as if they were claiming to have the same delicate feelings as ours. But later still, apropos of nothing in particular, my father was heard to remark: 'Well, I don't know, I'm damned if I know, but in any case he's a damned good driver.'" "He never lets you get away with anything," he had been accustomed to say with a kind of admiration of the Long One, who, in this instance, got away with murder. Incidentally, the slight value put upon a native's life is clear enough.

In "No Witchcraft for Sale" Gideon, the cook in the Farquhar family, displays another sort of skill. By using the root of a plant, he saves the eyesight of the little boy Teddy when a tree-snake spits venom into the child's eye. All the neighbors hear of it and are reminded of similar stories: "The bush is full of secrets. No one can live in Africa, or at least on the veld, without learning very soon that there is an ancient wisdom of leaf and soil and season—and, too, perhaps most important of all, of the darker tracts of the human mind—which is the black man's heritage." It was exasperating to the white man, "because while all of them knew that in the bush of Africa are waiting valuable drugs locked in bark, in simple-looking leaves, in roots, it was impossible to ever get the truth about them from the natives themselves."

Every effort is made to get the truth from old Gideon. Scientists come from town, with test tubes and chemicals. The Farquhars, religious people, share their God with Gideon, a mission-trained native, and their relations with him are friendly. But this time he is sullen and indifferent; he cannot remember the root; he is, they think, very unreasonable. Suddenly he appears to give in, and for a long hot morning he leads them all a merry chase through the bush, looking for the root. Finally he plucks at random some blue flowers and hands them to the scientist. It is days before the Farquhars and Gideon like each other again. In time it becomes a joke. "When are you going to show us the snake-root?" "But I did show you; you have forgotten."

The Magical drug would remain where it was, unknown and use-less, except for the tiny scattering of Africans who had the knowledge, natives who might be digging a ditch for the municipality in a ragged shirt and a pair of patched shorts, but who were still born to healing, hereditary healers, being the nephews or sons of the old witch doctors whose ugly masks and bits of bone and all the uncouth properties of magic were the outward signs of real power and wisdom.

The stories in which natives figure do not stress brutality or cruelty, and may even emphasize good intentions, as well as misunderstanding or indifference. Little Tembi is a piccannin whose life is saved by the nurse who marries a farmer and does all sorts of good deeds in the way of curing and teaching the natives. Tembi is for a time spoiled by her and comes to think of himself as privileged—and in the end he turns into a little delinquent, in spite of misdirected efforts to teach him better ways. One may conclude that the whole black-white pattern frustrates efforts at good will—or, simply, that juvenile delinquents turn up in any society.

Among the settlers in the district familiar to Doris Lessing in her childhood are English ex-army officers, like her father. Sometimes they are successful with their farms, like Major Gale, in "The De Wets Come to Kloof Grange"; sometimes, like Major Carruthers in "The Second Hut," they would do well enough except for some handicap. In his case, it is a sick wife—sick with heartbreak over the conditions they live in. She has long ago surrendered, and her only desire is for her husband to surrender, too—to go back home and take any job his brother could find for him. She has sunk into complete invalidism. To try to improve conditions on the farm, he hires an assistant, an Afrikaner, who is so desperately in need of a job—there had been a bad depression in the 1930's—that he conceals the fact that he has a wife and nine children until he has established them in the only lodging available—a hut little better than a dog kennel.

Unable to stand the spectacle of the swarming life in the hut, the major forces his boss-boy and workmen to build a second hut, depriving them, in his wish to house this family as soon as possible, of a customary holiday. So they are resentful. The assistant is good with cattle, but bad with natives; when the major is not around, he knocks them about, arousing further ill will that bides its time until the hut is nearly finished. Then the building mysteriously catches fire and burns, unfortunately killing the youngest baby. The major surrenders and writes to his brother, and his wife revives. The interest of the story is in the contrast between the English and the Afrikaner cultures—if one can say that this particular Afrikaner and his teeming wife have any culture, except a kind of animal warmth of affection. The natives despise about equally English and Afrikaners.

Major Gale, in contrast, is a successful farmer, and he and his wife have reared four sons, all now sailing the Seven Seas in the English Navy. Mrs. Gale lives in her middle age for the lovely garden she has created by years of toil—vivid English lawns, flowering African shrubs, water lilies and goldfish in a pond. She likes to sit on a ledge at the edge of her garden, looking off to the mountains and over the deep valley, with the river and the tropical jungle at the bottom. She has no love of the jungle, and she is surprised that the very young wife of the new assistant—an Afrikaner—likes to go down to the river and is not at all deterred by the presence of crocodiles. In her way this woman, too, is fond of nature.

This story has a feminist theme. Here are two totally different women, separated by age, culture, and class, isolated on the Rhodesian farm; their two husbands are absorbed in cattle and crops. Mrs. Gale manages the servants, keeps a perfect house, enjoys her garden, and is treated with the proper courtesy by her husband. She is appalled at the prospect of close contact with a girl who is, to her, a raw little barbarian, but she makes the proper advances. The girl, who lives with her husband in a cottage at some distance from the farm house, becomes very lonely, her marriage having been a hasty affair, with no pretense of romantic love. This man, De Wet, quite unfamiliar with the amenities dear to the Gales, is very blunt about the place of women; he is simply waiting for his bride to produce children and to stop bothering him with her needs and her moods. Mrs. Gale, at first just sorry for the girl, although annoyed at any approach to intimacy, begins to revert to an old sense of outrage at the way men ignore and disregard women.

When the two men are together, talking over their affairs, the major, for all his courtesy, shuts out his wife just as De Wet shuts out all women.

As the situation grows more uneasy, De Wet is convinced that "Mrs. Major" is making his wife discontented. And the girl acquires some of Mrs. Gale's attitudes. It builds up until the girl, to teach her husband a lesson, pretends to get lost on an evening walk. The veld is alive for hours with natives hunting with torches; the two men are frightened—for horrid things can happen in the African bush, as witness the killing of Leopard George's mistress—but, at the end, the girl appears from a hiding place in the house. Her husband knocks her around a bit. Mrs. Gale becomes hysterical. De Wet tells her to let his wife alone and orders Major Gale to take that woman out of here, "if you don't want me to beat her too."

De Wet is not presented as a brute—he is really kind; after it all, he tells his wife: "We just got mixed up, that's all." And Major Gale tells his wife: "He was just upset—it was no one's fault." And Mrs. Gale says: "Next time you get an assistant . . . get people of our kind. These might be savages, the way they behave."

A woman can be so lonely on one of those farms, and so starved for even the most miserable shreds and patches of cultural life, that the passing visits on business of a policeman or of an insurance salesman can be an event. "Lucy Grange" tells of such a woman. "The life of the farm, her husband's life, washed around the house, leaving old scraps of iron on the front steps where the children played wagon-and-driver, or a bottle of medicine for a sick animal on her dressing table among the bottles of Elizabeth Arden." An unattractive middle-aged insurance man calls one day, and stays to talk about pictures and books, and comes again during the hour when no one is around. They go to bed together. Though she doesn't really like him, she knows this will go on, because, as he says, "In a country like this we all learn to accept the second-rate."

A much more subtle study of loneliness in a Rhodesian setting is "Winter in July." The title suggests the spiritual and emotional atmosphere in which the three people involved live their lives: half-brothers, Tom and Kenneth, and Julia, Tom's wife. In Rhodesia, July is a winter month. The flowers of that season are the flowers of dryness; in the gusty winds, blossoms and leaves dance and shake; the essence of that time of year is "the essence of dry cold, of light thin sunshine, of high cold blue skies." The farm on the high veld is a successful one. During the war years, when Tom is in the army, Kenneth (rejected for service) manages it well. Julia, before marriage, had been for years a highly efficient secretary to important men in many parts of the world; in these wandering, restless years she had been rather like a man in her fear of being trapped into marriage. When she does marry Tom, and the three of them live comfortable lives in the attractive farmhouse, the two men somehow support her in their different manners. There is "a soft elastic tension" that binds them together.

It is a pleasant picture we see at the start—the three of them at supper on the veranda, lighted only by the lamp from the living room; through the pillars of the veranda "a full deep sky, holding a yellowy bloom from an invisible moon that absorbed the stars into a faint far glitter." Underneath the surface harmony one becomes aware, through Julia, of a kind of loss of feeling and of a question: what do our lives amount to? During Tom's absence on war service, Kenneth and Julia drift—one scarcely knows what word to use—into being lovers. (It was an odd feature of Rhodesian society during those years that a relationship like that of Julia and her brother-in-law was not made the subject of gossip—at least for the duration.) When Tom returns, "it seemed that in some perverse way the two men were brought even closer together for a time, by sharing the same woman." They don't feel what they ought to feel—and they know it. The evil in their lives is a loss of the capacity to feel—perhaps to "connect" (in E. M. Forster's well-known phrase).

The tension is snapped when Kenneth decides to marry an English girl, one of the marriageable women assisted to emigrate, as hopeful prospects for colonial matrimony. Julia could at least feel for this girl, as she observed the two men and listened to their plans—and "hated them, for the way they took their women into their lives, without changing a thought or a habit to meet them." She pictured the girl

arriving with nervous tact, hiding a longing for a home of her own, hoping not to find Julia an enemy. She would find not strife, or hostility or scenes—none of the situations which she might be prepared to face. She would find three people who knew each other so well that for the most part they found it hardly necessary to speak. She would find indifference to everything she really was, a prepared deliberate kindness. She would be like a latecomer to a party entering a room where everybody is already cemented by hours of warmth and intimacy. She would be helpless against Kenneth's need for her to be something she could not be: a young woman with the spiritual vitality to heal him.

There are several themes woven into this story, which, like most of Mrs. Lessing's longer stories, is developed in the direct manner of narrative, scene, dialogue. She is not much given to meticulous adherence to one angle of narration, but it is Julia in this story with whose viewpoint we become most familiar. It is the "not-feeling," rather than the loneliness, that is dominant, and, of course, the feminist theme is very evident. The locale happens to be Africa, and that is important chiefly because the woman on the isolated farms is so very restricted in her activities, once she has organized her household and her native servants. A man thinks that children will fill the gap in purposeful activity, though even then there are the ever-present native nursemaids; or if there are no children, a man thinks, as the brothers do in this story, that it will be very nice for his wife to have another woman around for companionship—any woman.

II *Men and Women*

In "Winter in July" and in a variety of other stories, long and short, it is the emotional ties, the subtle tensions, the shifts and changes in human relationships that capture Mrs. Lessing's curiosity. Her people do not usually fail to "connect," sometimes in very unusual ways. The title story of a recent volume is "A Man and Two Women." One of the novelettes in *Five* is *The Other Woman*, and that also might have been called "A Man and

Two Women." The scene is London, in wartime and after; and it all might have happened not long before Mrs. Lessing came to live in that house from which she pursued the English in 1949. One remembers Rose (*In Pursuit of the English*) speaking of the war period with a certain nostalgia; and Mrs. Lessing seems to have let her imagination play with the possible experiences of a working-class London girl, whose father might have been killed in the blitz, when their basement flat was almost buried under the ruins of the upper floors. This girl (another but quite different Rose) is helped by Jimmie on the night of the disaster. He finds her appealing in her bewilderment and helplessness—but, if he only knew it, she is far from helpless. Jimmie is a very kind fellow. While the war is going on, they are both busy at war jobs, their love-making has no prospect of permanence, and it is easy enough for Jimmie to be very vague about any ties he may already have. Actually he has been married and divorced, and he has to pay alimony for the support of his wife and two children—quite a drain on his resources. Rose thinks for a time that he is free to marry—and her eye is fixed on that goal—and then he admits that he is married, but leads her to think that his wife refuses to divorce him.

The war ends; Rose has saved a bit of money from her well-paid job; Jimmie has found her a habitable flat—quite a feat, but he was "essentially a man who knew people, got around, had irons in the fire and strings to pull." Rose furnishes it, and Jimmie stays there most of the time as *de facto* husband. They are often quite happy. Rose caters to his ulcers, and his ex-wife, whom he occasionally visits, is amused when she finds out that Rose tries to feed him properly—she herself couldn't care less. She knows all about Rose, but Rose is a long time finding out about her. There is also Pearl, the barmaid at the local pub, to whom Jimmie goes for consolation when the pressure of his ill-arranged affairs is too much. Rose had baffled her father by lapses into feminism, and she has the same effect on Jimmie. She is usually almost inarticulate, but she has her own ideas: "If I went to drink with a boy friend, you wouldn't like it . . . I don't like to go to pubs myself, but if I did, I don't see why not."

She does some reading of the newspapers, especially articles

like "Surplus Women Present Problem to the Churches."
"That's what I am," she says and laughs, to Jimmie's discom-
fort. Jimmie likes her to be childish and responsive. He doesn't
find funny what she sometimes laughs at. "I ask you if you're
happy and you laugh—what's funny about being happy?"
"Well, it stands to reason . . . people who talk about being
happy or unhappy, and then the long words—and the things
you say, women are like this, and men are like that, and polyg-
amous and all the rest, well . . . it just seems funny to me,"
she says lamely. For—and here Mrs. Lessing intervenes, as she
sometimes does—"she could have found no words at all for
what she felt, that deep knowledge of the dangerousness and
sadness of life. Bombs fell on old men, lorries killed people
(her mother had been killed by one) and the war went on and
on, and the nights when he did not come to her she would sit
by herself, crying for hours, not knowing why she was crying,
looking down from the high window, at the darkened, ravaged
streets."

Rose's father, an old Socialist, had tried to interest her in
politics, without success. "You're just like your mother. . . .
You haven't any logic." To arguments over who started the
war—"But, Rosie, Hitler's got to be stopped"—her reply is
simply that they all make her sick: Hitler and Roosevelt and
Churchill and Stalin and "your Atlee, too." Yet Rose does her
job in the munitions factory and her fire-watching, with "bewildered but patient courage." Once during the war she meets the
wife of the man she had almost married before her father had
been killed. Rose says it must be hard for her—husband at the
front, child to care for. And the woman replies that it will be
over some day—"when they've stopped playing soldiers." The
two women feel friendly in a shared basic contempt for men—
those children with their games. When Jimmie or her father
expresses some of his ideas, Rose often responds with a laconic
interrogative "Yes?" that is very disconcerting. "It was like a
statement of rock-bottom disbelief, a basic indifference to himself and the world of men. It was as if she said: There's only
one person I can rely on—myself."

In the end, Rose, having found out the truth about the divorced wife, writes to her to come to talk things over. The two

women in a scene of excellent comedy confront Jimmie. They are both still susceptible to his charm but fed up with his evasions and his drifting. They both know about Pearl, who may be pictured as waiting in the wings. Jimmie is going to be manoeuvred into the state he dreads—marriage and responsibility. He is surprised that Rose knows about Pearl—but she says that everyone knows: "There's my friend at the shop at the corner, who keeps my bit extra for me when there's biscuits or something going. He told me Pearl was crazy for you, and he said people said you were going to marry her." Mrs. Pearson, exwife, comments drily—"Just like him . . . He always thinks he's the invisible man."

Jimmie is reduced to a helpless "Jesus, women!" when he perceives that they want to see him tied up to Pearl. No one, says his ex-wife, is going to marry her, stuck with two kids, and she doesn't see why he shouldn't be tied up too; and on a sudden impulse, she says she will let him off the two pounds a week alimony, if he does marry Pearl. "Blackmail," says Jimmie, bitterly. Mrs. Pearson pats Rose's shoulders—Rose is crying—and says "There, now." And then she has another impulse: how would Rose like to come to live with her? She is going to start a little cake shop, having saved a bit during the war, and Rose can help her; there are three rooms and a kitchen; and the children are away at school during the day. For Mrs. Pearson is afraid that Rose will in the end succumb again to Jimmie's charm—which he is hopefully turning on again. And when Rose brings up a question very dear to her—her desire to adopt the orphaned little girl of the man she almost married—Mrs. Pearson with some reluctance agrees. Softened by this prospect, Rose tells Jimmie that, if he marries Pearl, she wouldn't mind letting him have the flat. And Mrs. Pearson thinks it isn't a bad idea. Jimmie is by now speechless. Mrs. Pearson makes it clear that, if he doesn't marry Pearl, he will have to go on paying her the two pounds a week alimony. It is touch and go at the last moment whether Jimmie will win Rose over to stay—he did love her after his fashion—but with Mrs. Pearson looking on, Rose holds out; the tension shifts and Rose "drooped away from him with a sigh"—he couldn't really love her, or he wouldn't have just sat there, watching her with his handsome grey eyes. "You won't regret it," says Mrs. Pearson. "Men—they're more trouble than they're worth. Women have to look after themselves these days."

In sharp contrast is "A Man and Two Women," the other story about a man and two women. It covers only a few hours. The married couple and the visiting woman friend, Stella, whose husband is away, have long been friends, very congenial, with common interests—painting and journalism—and an attitude of cool derision toward the rackets in both fields. They are very civilized people, and their conversation can imply much more than is said, since they know each other so well. But on this particular evening in the country cottage there is a little intruder—a baby, a rather late arrival in the life of the married pair. Their guest, who is older, has some trouble recalling what it was like when she had babies to deal with, what effect babies have on husbands, and so on. This baby has a very disturbing effect on all three of the adults, though it is as peaceful as a nursing kitten. It stirs up old emotions, provokes new ones, and very nearly upsets the delicate balance of the friendship. Something might have happened, but didn't. It was a near thing. Stella pulled back in time from the situation—though there was pleasure in the thought of blowing everything to bits—sending them all, including the baby, spinning down through the sky like "bits of debris after an explosion." "I'm going to miss my train if I don't go," she said. "Damn you both!" said her host—and accompanied her to the station. One spends a very interesting evening with these three and the baby, and is left reflecting upon pleasant evenings of conversation among old friends, when many things—memories, desires, possibilities—move under the agreeable familiar surface, and something might have happened.

There is great variety in the stories concerned with human relationships, whether brief encounters—with no particular significance in themselves, but successful in suggesting the flow of life around us—or long enduring, yet changing with the years, posing questions about what people mean to each other that may seem answered at a particular moment, but don't stay answered, and are perhaps unanswerable. Many of the brief encounters are sexual, occurring in the present or remembered. In "One off the Short List" a talented young woman theatrical designer lets herself be seduced by the ex-novelist who is interviewing her for a radio program. He wants only to prove his prowess, establish his masculine status publicly—and cross her off his list. She is aware of his motives and his tactics, and completely contemptuous. He succeeds and hates himself as a failure. In "Each Other" a brother and sister seem to have strayed out of the primitive world of Wagner's *Ring* into a London flat to carry on a love affair, which is, curiously enough, not revolting. In "Wine" a man and a woman, old acquaintances, no longer young, meet in a Paris café, and each recalls an experience out of the past. He talks, she remembers. His memory, from his student days, is explicit and clear, of a gay student expedition into the country, during which he had refused one of the young girls who had offered herself to him. The woman, whose own memory is of an undefined frustration vaguely associated with a moonlit landscape—she does not tell what it is—feels angry with him for rejecting the girl, who all her life would remember this rejection. In "The Woman," two elderly men at a Riviera resort exchange over their luncheon dubiously accurate amorous reminiscences that seem to involve the same woman.

In "A Woman on a Roof," a good-looking woman, sunbathing on a London roof among the chimney pots on a rare hot summer day and indifferent to any possible observers, is descried by three workmen who are repairing the gutters: Harry, middle-aged and tolerant; Stanley, newly married and excitable, who doesn't like to think of his wife's exposing herself like that; and Tommy, seventeen, imaginative and susceptible. The work they are doing in the heat makes the indifference of the woman—even when she becomes aware of their whistles—particularly irritating. Tommy hates her and loves her and imagines alluring encounters with her. There are several days of this, building up into an experience for Tommy—more and more remote from any possible reality. Finally—his companions having gone home one afternoon to escape the heat—Tommy makes his way to her rooftop, a scarlet-faced, excited boy; and he stammers out his desire to make her acquaintance.

She tries ignoring him, and then tells him that if he gets a kick from seeing women in bikinis, why not take a six-penny ride to the Lido (in Hyde Park). He remembers how nice she had been in his dreams. When, the next day, it rains, he thinks, viciously, "Well, that's fixed you!"

Two ladies of an old, if not the oldest, profession discuss their problems in "Between Men"; the conversation is very practical, very enlightening and entertaining, but it doesn't contain Mrs. Lessing's best kind of humor. These and other stories of the brief encounter variety are lighthearted for the most part. In "Road to the Big City"—Johannesburg—a journalist, passing through, becomes interested in two sisters from the country, one who is already at home in the corruption of the city and the other who has just come to join her. Janson tries unsuccessfully to persuade her to go back home. Not that it matters very much, this surrender to a compassionate impulse.

Other stories, slight on the surface, give us passing moments of awareness. They are not charged with the significance of Virginia Woolf's well-known "moments," but they contribute to the total impression of what it is like to be alive, not in crises and at turning points, but just in the ordinary way of being young and then not so young and then old, and of discovering along the way things about living that cannot be understood until they are felt. Some of these moments are made beautiful in Mrs. Lessing's world by sensory images associated with the experience. In "Flight" an old man, resenting both his age and the youth of his granddaughter and her young man, watches them returning to the farm from a lovers' walk. They bring him a pigeon, for he is something of a pigeon fancier. With a sharp change of mood, he releases the pet pigeon he has been playing with, and in that act he releases himself from his resentment. The pigeon joins others in a flight, as he watches: they "wheeled in a wide circle, tilting their wings so there was flash after flash of light, and one after another they dropped from the sunshine of the upper sky to shadow, one after another returning to the shadowy earth over trees and grass and field, returning to the valley and the shelter of night."

We turn from age to youth, to Catherine, aged thirteen: she has two experiences one day, when taken on a visit to her fifteen-year-old friend Philip at his school. They see a film about criminals and capital punishment; and she tries to read a story from a book Philip likes, finds the author, Isaac Babel, very old—he has been dead twenty years—and very remote from her interests, but persists in asking questions of the lady who had taken her on the visit. A week later, in a charming letter thanking the lady for the most lovely day in her whole life, she writes that the film had demonstrated to her beyond the shadow of a doubt that "Capital Punishment is a Wicked Thing"; that she had been meditating about Isaac Babel, and now she sees that "the conscious simplicity of his style is what makes him, beyond the shadow of a doubt, the great writer that he is." "P.S. Has Philip said anything about my party? I wrote but he hasn't answered. . . . I hope he comes, because sometimes I feel I shall die if he doesn't." ("Homage for Isaac Babel")

III *Beyond the Personal*

Totally different in mood from any of the stories of human relationships that we have been discussing is "Dialogue." It reaches far beyond the personal experience of the man and woman involved into a bleak impersonal world of speculation about our lives. Two visual impressions—two images—adumbrate the meaning: the shabby, crowded London street along which the woman walks to the tall building where her invalid friend lives in a tower room, and the tower room where they talk for an hour or so and where an unspoken dialogue goes on between them. They have long been friends—once they were lovers. And he has lived with pain for a long time.

Rather dreading the visit, she lingers on her way among the women marketing in the busy high street, listens to the conversations around the vegetable stalls, to Ada and Fred exchanging notes about rheumatism, as if it were a wild beast, until she could positively see it, "a jaguar-like animal crouched to spring behind the brussels sprouts." She disciplines herself against the cheerful response of her blood to the small familiar busyness of the street by reminding herself that Ada is repulsive and fat and Fred stupid and that the boy and girl standing in front of the music shop have a future that can be guessed at by "the sharply aggressive yet forlorn postures of shoulders and loins." It was all squalid and pathetic, but "what of it, insisted her blood." She smiles, and the smile invites jokes and cheerful comments from passersby. Why does she feel this serenity, after forty, after years of pretty violent emotion? Would it continue? Why should it? "Possibly this was a room in her life, she had walked into it, found it furnished with joy and well-being, and would walk through and out again into another room, still unknown and unimagined." She leaves the street with its old houses, its "small, shallow, litter of building," goes up in the lift to the top floor of the tall apartment house, and rings at door 39. A little dizzy from the swift upward movement of the lift, she feels a "moment's oneness" with Bill, who opens the door, using the handle as a support.

Bill's close-cut reddish hair fits like a cap; he has a face "where every feature strove to dominate, where large calm green eyes just held the balance with a mouth designed, apparently, only to express the varieties of torment." His bedroom is curtained and dark. But the main room, where they sit—he in the specially constructed chair which he can manipulate—is large, high, airy, the colors black and white and red, and one wall virtually all glass. From that window London is seen as from an airplane. The room is like an "exposed platform swaying in the clouds." The surface talk is about books, music, people they know; he plays some jazz records. Underneath, an old argument goes on, sometimes breaking out into words. Why did he choose to be so isolated, so disconnected? Why not the warmth of a family, marriage if possible, comfort, other people? "Never isolation, never loneliness, not the tall windbattered room where the sky showed through two walls. But he refused common sense. 'It's no good skirting around what I am, I've got to crash right through it, and if I can't, whose loss is it?' " She had not been strong enough to crash through what she most feared. But, he says, "You have a choice, I haven't, unless I want to become a little animal living in the fur of other people's warmth."

They are two different people who can, at rare moments,

make contact. And since their minds often move together in this odd dialogue, he sometimes answers what she has not said, as, for instance, "I don't understand the emotions, except through my intelligence, *normality* never meant anything to me until I knew you. . . ." She tries to see them in this room, this insecure platform in height, "tenacious against storm and rocking foundations," as if a third eye were watching them, two little people, "as she had seen the vegetable sellers, the adolescents, the woman whose husband had rheumatism, . . . sitting there together in silence on either side of the tall room, and the eye seemed to expand till it filled the universe with disbelief and negation." She acknowledges that she is "split," that what she thinks contradicts what she feels, that it is all meaningless, an accident, "but all the same, everything gives me pleasure all the time." And suppose it is a contradiction, why should she care? He calls her, and those like her, flies buzzing in the sun. "Suppose," he says, "that *I* am the future? . . . It seems to me that I am. Suppose the world fills more and more with people like me, then—" "The little flies will have to buzz louder." "It seems to me that the disconnected like me," he says, "must see more clearly than you people." She goes to the great window; and he gets out of his chair, stands beside her, supporting himself with hand on the sill; far below in the streets the lights have come on, "making small yellow pools and gleams on pavements where the tiny movements of people seemed exciting and full of promise. . . . She stood silent, feeling the life ebbing and coiling along the pavements and hoping he felt it." Then they sit in the gathering dusk, in a strange mood, until she says, "For God's sake turn the light on."

When she left him, the street was unfamiliar to her. "The hazy purple sky that encloses London at night was savage, bitter, and the impulse behind its shifting lights was a form of pain. . . . The people passing were hostile, stupid animals from whom she wished to hide herself. . . ." The scene she walked through had a flat, black-and-white, two-dimensional, jagged look. It was a projection of her own mind: there was no life in it save what she could breathe in it. "And she herself was dead and empty, a cardboard figure in a flat painted set of streets." Why should it not all come to an end? "The tall building, like a black tower, stood over her, kept pace with her, it was not possible to escape from it."

Her hand picked a leaf from a hedge. As she fingered it, a faint pungent smell came to her nostrils; as she lifted it, it seemed to explode "with a vivid odour into the senses of her brain so that she understood the essence of the leaf and through it the scene she stood in." She stood fingering the leaf, while life came back: "The pulses were beating again." An elderly woman passed, mysterious in the half-light, and smiled at her. But the dark tower kept pace with her—"high, narrow, terrible, all in darkness save for a light flashing at its top where a man, held upright by the force of his will, sat alone staring at a cold sky in vertiginous movement." As she moved steadily on, with one hand "she secretly touched the base of the tower whose shadow would always follow her now, challenging her, until she dared to climb it. With the other hand she held fast to the leaf."

The grim view of a possible future is symbolized by the dark tower of "Dialogue." The evil is shadowy and undefined, perhaps only the creation of a mood. But the evil of "The Eye of God in Paradise" is sharp and concrete and of recent memory. This story is one of the few with a setting outside Africa and England. Two British doctors—Mary, a children's specialist, and Hamish, a specialist in geriatrics—are taking together a three weeks' unconventional and economical vacation in Bavaria in 1951. Mary's fiancé had been killed over Germany in the war, and Hamish's German wife had disappeared during a rescue mission in Germany. They are not looking for clues—this is not a suspense story—but their interest in what they see is sharp and critical and their vacation mood is easily disturbed. They go to a winter tourist center at the lower end of a valley that runs up to the barrier of the snow mountains, a place popular with now prosperous Germans and affluent Americans. Its tourist attractions are fully exploited, with folk singing, peasant costumes, and so on.

There is a scene in a restaurant patronized by Germans, some in family groups, healthy and bronzed, hearty eaters; and another in a night club, where a singer subtly insults these obviously British conquerors in one of his ballads, to the pleasure of his audience. One is reminded of two of Thomas Mann's stories—*Mario and the Magician* and *Death in Venice*—in which the holiday atmosphere also has undertones that are sinister and threatening; and there is a further resemblance to *Mario* in the almost hypnotic effect produced on the two doctors by a German doctor with a face like a mask created by skin grafting after war wounds. This Dr. Schroeder forces himself upon them, and they are unresisting because of their mingled repulsion, compassion, and sense of guilt. He manoeuvres them into changing their lodgings and their plans. Of course he wishes to use them in helping him get to England. Their victimization is completely believable. They are worried, besides, by their "complicated and irrational" dislike of the healthy German family they observe in the restaurant.

All the details of the gay setting are enhanced by such sinister intrusions as the legless beggar at the door of the restaurant.

Inside was a long room sheltered by glass on two sides from the snow which could be seen spinning down through the areas of yellow light conquered from the black mass of the darkness by the room and its warmth and its noise and its people. It was extraordinarily pleasant to enter this big room, so busy with pleasure and to see the snow made visible only during its passage through the beams from the big windows, as if the wilderness of the mountain valley had been admitted just so far as would give the delight of contrast to the guests who could see the savagery as a backdrop of pretty spinning white flakes.

They escape briefly from Dr. Schroeder's supervision to a *gemütlich* little cottage way up toward the snows. Then they go to a nearby war-damaged city to see a doctor in charge of a mental hospital, with whom Hamish had had a slight prewar contact. Their value had risen in Dr. Schroeder's estimation when he learned of this connection. The ruined city—it was British bombs that had done the damage—is in sharp contrast to the holiday ski resort; the crowds waiting at the bus stop are very different from the holiday makers; and Dr. Kroll—conservative, aristocratic, who speaks of the "upstart" Hitler—is the opposite of the repulsive Dr. Schroeder. But they had learned from Dr. Schroeder that Dr. Kroll sometimes spent months locked up in his own hospital during fits of deep depression; then he painted the remarkable pictures in oils with which the corridors are lined—some gay with brilliant colors, others macabre. Dr. Kroll takes them through some of the wards, where there are deformed and mentally ill children. A five-year-old boy in a strait jacket haunts Mary. What was it like under Hitler? But Dr. Kroll is uncommunicative. One of the most remarkable paintings, in clear blues and greens, is of a forest with sparkling streams, brilliant birds, and luxuriant plants. But from the center of the sky glares a large black eye. It is as if the doctor had painted his fantasy paradise, and then, looking at it in some fit of misery, had painted in "that black condemnatory, judging eye." He tells them that he calls the painting "the eye of God in Paradise." "You like it?" And he gives them a photograph of it.

They go back to the bus stop, through the ruins, the grey and dirty snow; they pass the bomb craters, the half-constructed new building; they hear the throbbing of the machines at work; they see the patient queues, and join the waiting crowd. "Behind the ruined buildings rose the shapes and outlines of the city that had been destroyed, and the outlines of the city that would be rebuilt. It was as if they stood solid among the ruins and ghosts of dead cities and cities not yet born." The faces of the people about them, waiting, seemed to become transparent and fluid. "The dead of two wars peopled the ruined square and jostled the living—a silent snowbound multitude. . . ." They thought of the dead, "huddled up, silent, patient under the snow"; they listened to the silence "under which seemed to throb from the depths of the earth the memory of the sound of marching feet, of heavy, black-booted marching feet."

IV *Lighter Moods of Irony and Fantasy*

"Dialogue" and "The Eye of God in Paradise" are stories of unusual distinction, imaginative and thought-provoking. The range of interest in Doris Lessing's stories and the variety of moods are impressive. Considering her political commitments, what would one expect from "The Day Stalin Died"? What one gets is an amusing chronicle of a day in London, told in the first person, during which the news of Stalin's death is just another headline. The narrator has things to do: engagements to keep, little decisions to make, bits of conversation to carry on with taxicab drivers, bus conductors, photographers, Aunt Emma and Cousin Jessie to meet, coming in from the country for an appointment with a photographer. And, while all this activity is going on, her mind is busy in the disjointed fashion in which minds work under such conditions. She has had to put off a date with Bill, an American film writer who has been black-listed and who is divorcing his wife after twenty years; she—the narrator—is planning to introduce him to Beatrice, an old friend from South Africa whose passport has expired and who —having been named as a Communist—can't go back. She had fancied Bill and Beatrice might have much in common. But "later it turned out that they disapproved of each other." (The chronicle now takes on a reminiscent tone: Beatrice thought that Bill was corrupt because he wrote sexy comedies for televi-sion under another name and acted in bad films, and she saw no justification in the apology that a guy must eat.) Before the narrator can meet Cousin Jessie, she has to see her comrade Jean, who for many years has been a self-appointed guide to-ward a correct political viewpoint, and who has pointed out that one of the narrator's recent stories "gave an incorrect anal-ysis of the class struggle" and that one of her recent remarks at a meeting savored of flippancy—a remark that there seemed to be evidence for supposing "that a certain amount of dirty work must be going on in the Soviet Union." Jean, the daughter of a bishop, has warned her against the pressure of the forces of capitalist corruption on intellectuals. But she reflects: "I could not help feeling that there were times when the capitalist press, no doubt inadvertently, spoke the truth." One feels Stalin lurk-ing off stage all day.

Readers who dislike any light treatment of serious politics would object to the little scene in "Outside the Ministry." At ten in the morning, on the London pavement, among the pass-ing clerks and typists and the fat pigeons, two young Africans, of different political views, are waiting for their respective leaders to keep an appointment with Her Majesty's Minister. They carry on a dialogue full of political allusions, first with each other, and then with their leaders. Their animosities and

rivalries and intrigues—which include hints of attempts on op-
ponents' lives—are very politely displayed, with many graceful
flourishes and with an occasional exchange of delighted smiles
of awareness at political absurdities. In this duel there are some
very clever thrusts. These emergent African politicos are regret-
tably like other politicians. The scene, so sharply and amusingly realized in speech and gesture, would be delightful screen
entertainment.

"A Letter from Home" indirectly implies that the kind of
censorship of ideas that notoriously exists in Suid Afrika might
develop paranoia in a liberally minded young Afrikaans poet.
This is an interesting experiment in using Afrikaans idiom or
dialect. An English-speaking Afrikaner writes to a friend about
a poet they had both known years before at the university they
attended. This Johannes Potgiester had published poems while
he had some sort of job at the university, and was attacked by
the heresy-hunters; as he was no fighter, he resigned and went
to live with his Tantie Gertrude in a "godforsaken dorp" in the
Orange Free State. Some years later the narrator visits him,
and finds him tyrannized over by his fat Zulu cook Esther, who
watches out for his spiritual as well as his physical welfare.
While she is away at the Kaffir church on Sunday, the old
friends relax, and the poet shows the poems he has written in a
strange script: a kind of chronicle of the lives of the citizens of
Blagspruit—"the same everywhere in the world, but worse in
Suid Afrika and worse a million times in Blagspruit."

It is fine poetry, but the poet is frightened at the bare sugges-
tion that his friend should take it away and have it published.
It is even dangerous to keep it around; both drunk now, they
take the manuscript and go out under the moon into the veld;
and there, the devil aiding them, they find a thorn-tree. "All
virgin it was, its big black spikes lifted up and shining in the
devil's moon. And we wept a long time more, and we tore out
the pages from his manuscript and we made them into little
screws of paper and we stuck them all over the thorns." And
then they sat under the tree in the moonlight, "the black spikey
thorns making thin purplish shadows all over us and over the
white sand. Then we wept for the state of our country and
the state of poetry." The next morning Johannes is out on the

windy veld chasing after screws of paper whirling around in the dust. Suppose the predicant or the mayor got their hands on them? The friend tries to persuade him that, even if they did, they couldn't read the script, and won't he let the poems he has rescued be published in *Onwards?* "No, no, do you want them to kill me?" Later the friend gets a letter from Hans, in ordinary writing but rather unformed and wild, saying that he is leaving the place; they know him and look at him, and he is going North to the river.

The thorn-tree was prepared for by a little episode on their walk earlier in the afternoon. It was a butcherbird's cache, and every thorn had a beetle or a worm or something stuck on it; one big brown beetle, waving its legs in the air, finally freed itself; and then, to the friend's amazement, the poet picked it up and stuck it back on the thorn. "The ants would have killed it, just look!" The ground was swarming with ants, so there was logic in it. "Well, it was Sunday, and no bars open. I took a last look at the beetle, the black thorn through its oozing middle, waving its black legs at the setting sun, and I said: 'Back home, Hans, and to hell with Esther, we're going to get drunk.'" I suppose the impaled beetle is the poet.

Mrs. Lessing's usual direct narrative manner focuses the reader's attention on the happenings and the people. She does little experimenting with techniques, but uses, very expertly, the well-tried forms. But there are quite a number of exceptions that suggest future development in her art. In these stories she may be trying to convey something that slips through the nets that catch the usual meanings. She is quite an accomplished dreamer—as we have noted; but she does not use dreams as often in her stories as we might expect. When she does, it is in an unusual way. "A Room" and "Two Potters" (in the 1963 collection) are examples.

Rooms have a special meaning for Doris Lessing. She has lived in many, but only the one in the farmhouse on the veld is "home." They assume almost the significance of a symbol—like the tower room in "Dialogue." One of the rooms she (the narrator) lived in for a time in London had had many previous occupants, about whom inquiries were often made; the ceiling was not soundproof and she could hear the movements of the elderly Swedish couple in the flat overhead. Sometimes she knew the old woman was taking an afternoon nap, as she herself often did; and she liked to think of them both, lying horizontally, as if on two shelves. Afternoon sleep is more interesting than night sleep: "I always drift off to sleep in the afternoon with the interest due to a long journey into the unknown . . . and the sleep is thin and extraordinary and takes me to regions hard to describe in a waking state." But one afternoon the sleep was so different that she thought she was awake. The room seemed larger; there was a small smoking iron grate instead of her bronze gas fire; and other details suggested that it was the same room but in an earlier phase of occupancy. There was an atmosphere of thin poverty. Sounds of a quarrel drifted in from the outside, and a hostile laugh came from the floor above; and she felt—for she was there in the room—"desolate with a loneliness that felt it would never be assuaged." "I was a child, I knew that. And that there was a war . . . war had something to do with this dream, or memory —whose?" Coming back to herself, in the familiar room, she tried to dream herself again into that other room—which was under hers, or beside it, or "existing in someone's memory"— perhaps a frightened small child's; he or she "must have been very small for the room to look so big."

Was the dream suggested by a fancy Mrs. Lessing owed to her young son? In "London Diary," conributed by Mrs. Lessing to the *New Statesman* in March, 1958, among the London items picked up in courtrooms and laundries and supermarkets is a bit of dialogue with the little boy, down with the flu in one of those transient rooms. He likes the thoughts he has when his temperature is up, and he wonders what will happen to these thoughts when he leaves: "Will they stay here and get into the minds of the people who come next?"

"Two Potters" is really three potters: one who made pots in Africa—whom the narrator had known; one who was an Englishwoman, Mary Tawnish, who lived in a village, was married to a schoolteacher and had three boys; and one who appeared in a dream. Perhaps to provoke Mary Tawnish, who used to say that she never had a dream in her life, the narrator described this potter-dream in one of her letters to Mary. The old potter lived in a settlement of baked mud houses, half finished, half crumbling away, set down in a vast plain of reddish earth, ringed by distant hazy mountains. There sat the old man with his potter's wheel, "with the hundreds of pots and dishes drying in rows on the straw, dipping his hand into an enormous jar of water and scattering drops that smelt sweet as they hit the dust and pitted it." The dream has the sharp visual quality characteristic of Mrs. Lessing's writing. The narrator wonders what the old potter would think of Mary's strange colored bowls and jugs which she sold to the big shops in London.

We all have recurrent dreams, but the dreams about the potter, which continue, do not merely recur but develop. The settlement grows bigger, people appear in the market place; shadows from great birds drift over the plain; a small boy crouches by the potter watching every move he makes. Mary begins to play the game with the narrator, in her practical way, writing that she is glad the old man now has some customers; that there ought to be a well in the settlement, which is obviously short of water; and that it is time the potter used some color. But the dreamer replies that she isn't responsible for the settlement—that is how things are in that place. After quite an interval she dreams again, and again there are changes; she sees the plain, now all populated, as if from the mountains, which have come closer in, reaching up tall and blue into blue sky. In the dream she floats down from the mountain and finds the old potter, still creating his pots.

But the next dream is discouraging; the potter's hands are still; she knows—in the dream—what he is thinking. And she writes to Mary that the old man is tired with long centuries of making pots whose life is so short; "the litter of broken pots under the settlement had raised its level twenty feet by now, and every pot had come off his wheel. He wanted God to breathe life into his clay rabbit. He had hoped to see it lift up its long red-veined ears, to feel its furry feet on his palm, and watch it hop down and off among the great earthenware pots, sniffing at them and twitching its ears—a live thing among the forms of clay." Mary replies that the old man is getting above himself, and, anyway, wouldn't a cow be more useful than a rabbit in that settlement? The dreamer replies that she can't do anything about that settlement when she is dreaming it, but when she is awake—well, why not bring the rabbit to life? The poor old man deserves one; so the rabbit hops off the old man's hand into the dust.

In a delightfully convincing way the dream fantasy breaks through into reality. The dreamer doesn't hear from Mary. "I knew it was because of my effrontery in creating that rabbit, inserting myself into the story." So she writes to Mary, building up a little tale about what might have happened if it had been Mary who dreamed about the potter, and how she might have made a rabbit, secretly, and taken it into the field. . . . Mary replies practically that the rabbits, having become a pest in England, were eliminated by the virus myxomatosis; but she had made several in blue and green glaze for her younger boys because they had never seen a live rabbit. And the youngest had put his blue rabbit in a hedge, and Farmer Smith had shot it to pieces in the dusk. There were consequences that play themselves out amusingly when the narrator visits the Tawnishes over a week end. The rabbit had come alive in the little boy's fancy; and, as revenge on the farmer, he imagines setting fire to his house. He insists he did it. It all works up into a little family comedy—as lively and real as the dreams were.

But the most interesting detail holding the dream and reality together is the little creature Mary has fashioned for the dream potter: a sort of rabbit or hare, "but with ears like neither—narrower, sharp, short, like the pointed unfolding shoots of a plant. It had a muzzle more like a dog's than a rabbit's. . . ." In short, it was adapted to the conditions of the settlement in the plain. "It looked like a strangely shaped rock, or like the harsh, twisted plants that sometimes grow on rocks." When the narrator says that it isn't the creature she had seen on the potter's palm, the practical Mary says, "What was an English rabbit doing there at all?" The dreamer thanks Mary for humoring her—for coming down to her level long enough to play games with her. Mary humors her husband and children in the same way. The character of Mary shows in the way she straightens out the complications in the situation created by the farmer's shooting the boy's rabbit. She is most efficient, but rather irritatingly superior. She has condescended to the dreamer.

The dreamer takes the odd clay creature back with her to London. And that night she dreams herself into the market place and gives it to the old potter, who scatters water upon it. The creature jumps off and away, clear of the settlement, to some jagged brown rocks, "where it raised its front paws and froze in the posture Mary had created for it." The old potter goes back to work and the small boy crouches watching, "and the water flung by the potter's right hand sprayed the bowl he was making and the child's face in a beautiful curving spray of glittering light."

A parable of the creative gift?

V *Around the Bend: Case Histories*

There is a small group of stories that deal with abnormal people, and it will be interesting to see what part such people play in the long novels—if any. "Plants and Girls," a strange fantasy of a subnormal boy, ending in murder, while not quite believable, is quite horrifying. The boy is obsessed by a tree in front of the house in an African town where he lives with his mother. It is an old tree, a survivor from the veld; and he thinks of it as coming up through layers of rubble from the breathing soil and from the underground rivers. He stretches his fingers like roots toward the earth. The neighbor children call him "Moony," but one girl from a big family across the street tries to draw him into the normal circle and to play with him. To embrace her or to embrace the tree—it makes no difference to him. His mother dies, the tree is cut down, he lives on in the house under some sort of guardianship, and a young sapling takes the place of the old tree in his fantasy. In time the youngest girl of the family across the way—her sisters all married—is lonely enough to feel toward the boy something between compassion and an unhealthy attraction. For him, the girl is as the sapling, and he wishes somehow to get at the source of her being; her bones, her hair, her blood are as the trunk, the leaves, the sap of the tree. When they lie embraced behind the hedge, he probes with his fingers into her flesh, trying to reach the bone of her arm, the joint of her shoulder. Though she resists, she is drawn back again and again, until he kills her. There is the sort of doomed attraction between them that drew together Moses and Mrs. Turner in *The Grass Is Singing*, but the outcome is less convincing.

Recurring to the fancy that a room might retain the thoughts of an occupant and that these thoughts might enter the dreams of a later occupant, one would prefer not to go to sleep in Room Nineteen. "To Room Nineteen" is a long story, told very soberly, almost like a case history; it follows a straight line of development from normality to insanity and suicide. The "case" is Susan Rawlings, the wife and mother in a comfortable, prosperous marriage, living in a nice house with a garden on the Thames near Richmond. The opening sentence announces that it is a story about "a failure in intelligence: the Rawlings' marriage was grounded in intelligence." Intelligence takes a hard beating in the story. It seems to prevent those consciously addicted to intelligent behavior from quarrelling, sulking, getting angry; they are silent when they ought to burst into speech and make accusations; and "above all, intelligence forbids tears." The Rawlings "used their intelligence to preserve what they had created from a painful and explosive world: they looked around them and took lessons. All around them, marriages collapsing, or breaking, or rubbing along (even worse, they felt). They must not make the same mistakes." But there is something more than too much reliance on intelligence at work to account for Susan's collapse, which is a slow drifting from boredom—after her four children are launched into their school years—through a phase of feeling that she had for years signed herself over to other people and did not know what her essential self was—as if she had been in cold storage; and then to irrational fears, strongest when she is in her garden alone. There are intermissions when she goes through familiar routines of family life; and little departures from normal habits, like wanting a room entirely to herself, are, after some surprise, accepted by children and husband and housekeeper.

The restlessness, the emptiness, begin to seem to her like a demon to be kept at bay. Finally the demon comes to life in the garden. Her terrors have crystallized around this fantastic figure who wants to get into her and take her over. And so she tries to escape and takes a room in town in a miserable little hotel, just for certain days every week; there she can be alone, with no one knowing where she is. Naturally she has to tell lies at home, and naturally her husband begins to suspect she has a lover and tracks her down to the address in Paddington. And since she would prefer that he did think her strange state meant a secret lover, she is led to invent one, helped by the fact that her husband admits to having a mistress. Before she reaches this state, she had become two persons, leading two separate lives. Three times a week for a full day in Room Nineteen in dingy Fred's Hotel, she sat and did nothing, and had no past and no future, felt "emptiness run deliciously through her veins like the movement of her blood." But when she had been searched out, she could no longer find peace in Room Nineteen; she was like an addict suddenly deprived. And when her husband, doing his best to be intelligent and rational, thinks maybe now he and his mistres and she, with her mythical lover (she gives him a name and profession, but says he is out of town) could make a foursome—develop one of those intricate relationships of "civilized tolerance" in a "charming afterglow of autumnal passion"—she realizes she has reached the end of the road. Back in Room Nineteen, she breathes the gas into her lungs and drifts off into the dark river.

The length of the story permits a convincing build-up of the house and garden, the contrasting dinginess of the rundown hotel, the change in the relations of husband and wife, the stages of the mental breakdown. Perhaps there is social criticism of cushioned lives?

"Notes for a Case History" is not told in case-history manner, except in a brief opening describing Maureen Watson's early childhood as a "social viewer" might have written it. I suppose Maureen's story is typical of hundreds of other stories that might be told of a pretty girl growing up after the war in a London neighborhood of petty shopkeepers, pretty enough to make her mother ambitious for her to come up in the world, by way of a secretarial school and a typist's job in an architect's office. Her destination—provided she managed her capital well, that is, her beauty and her virginity—was a marriage into a better class. The point of the story is how she almost made it, always with her eye on the main chance, but lost out, ironically enough, because of a lapse into integrity. Maureen's career belongs in the world Doris Lessing began to explore in her pursuit of the English—especially the English working class; and it has the convincing detail that comes from close and sympathetic observation, and from an ear for dialogue.

VI *Class Attitudes*

"England versus England" is a more ambitious venture into the subject of class attitudes. Charlie Thornton, the brilliant son of a mining family in a village in the north near Doncaster, comes from Oxford, where he is a student, to spend a few days with his family, whom he has not seen for nearly a year. He is close to a serious nervous breakdown, just before examinations. The theme is conveniently summed up in a leaflet which Charlie, a week before his visit home, had taken to the doctor at the university who had written it, a doctor provided by the college authorities as a father-figure to advise on personal problems. The title is: "A Report into the Increased Incidence of Breakdown Among Undergraduates." Charlie had underlined these sentences: "Young men from working-class and lower middle-class families on scholarships are particularly vulnerable. For them the gaining of a degree is obviously crucial. In addition they are under the continuous strain of adapting themselves to middle-class mores that are foreign to them. They are victims of a clash of standards, a clash of cultures, divided loyalties."

To present Charlie, not as a statistic or a case, but as a human being, with the background of his village and his family, the village pub, the doctor's office, and the compartment in the train that is taking him back to London—that is the storyteller's problem. And this storyteller, being a feminist, makes a good deal of Charlie's mother and the way Charlie resents the kind of life she has had to lead—one taken for granted by her family and by herself. I am not entirely convinced that it is Charlie whose emotions have made him perceive all these things about a woman's life in the past and present of a mining village—rather, it may be Doris Lessing coaching Charlie. How accurately Mrs. Lessing has caught the accents and idioms of differing class vocabularies in this story must be left to the experts to decide. But the human quality typical of all her writing makes Charlie and his family seem authentic. We hope he didn't have that breakdown.

In a broadcast over the BBC (repeated October 8, 1963, over the New York station WBAI) Mrs. Lessing commented on the English class system, as she had come to see it after leaving Southern Rhodesia, where the whites were a minority and couldn't afford class divisions in a color-divided society. In London, living in working-class streets, she found some of the class attitudes very odd—funny—but not to the English; and she marveled at what the "lower classes" put up with— grumbling, but accepting. A good place for a writer, these streets she lived in. In "London Diary" in the *New Statesman,* March, 1958, she calls herself a "compulsive eavesdropper," picking up stories at the market and the laundry and on the buses and even in police courts—for she has done her bit in political demonstrations.

In the Preface to *African Stories,* Doris Lessing expresses the hope that the stories will be read with as much pleasure as she had in writing them. "Some writers I know have stopped writing short stories because, as they say, 'there is no market for them.' Others like myself, the addicts, go on, and I suspect would go on even if there really wasn't any home for them but a private drawer." The enjoyment she has in writing them, market or not, helps to explain the great variety of the more than fifty which have been published. One hopes those in the private drawer may also find a market.

CHAPTER 4

The Novels

I *Retreat to Innocence*

*R*etreat to Innocence, Doris Lessing's fourth novel to be
published after she left Southern Rhodesia for England in
1949, came out in March, 1956. Since she had started on her
seven-weeks' return visit to Southern Rhodesia in that month, it
must have been written in 1955; and it was her first full-length
novel with an English setting, although not all the characters
are English. Jan Brod is a Central European exile, and so are
several of his friends. Politics complicate the love affair between Jan and Julia, the young upper-class English girl, whose
father, Sir Andrew Barr, has an inherited business which he
leaves to his partner to run, confining his own activities to pre-
siding over Board meetings. He enjoys an agreeable life as amateur of the arts, including the gastronomic, and has a place in
Norfolk, and clubs and ladies in London. His second wife,
Julia's mother, had been divorced, and so had Sir Andrew; and
both of them are widely tolerant of behavior and of ideas, leaving their daughter and Andrew's son by his first marriage to
pursue their own paths, feeling much affection for them, but
very little responsibility. Julia had had some education, but was
not interested in entering a university. She had learned short-
hand and typing, since her mother—who votes Labour—
thought she had better have some skills she could earn a
living by. She is twenty-one, enchantingly pretty, living in a flat
in the West End with her friend Betty, who is not pretty, but is
by no means unenterprising or without resources. Both of them
are taking courses in something. But at the moment it is summer and a pleasant one by some chance; the parks are delightful; the espresso bars—the Green Parrot, or the Old Danube—
each with its special clientèle, have the relaxed atmosphere of
European cafés. Not all the young men are on vacation. Julia's

young man, Roger, who is something in the Home Office, takes
Julia rather for granted at the beginning, but finds her more
desirable at the end.

Julia, like other rather spoiled members of her generation in
the 1950's, as Mrs. Lessing saw them, is reacting against the
casual sex attitudes of her parents' generation, but on the surface she is sophisticated about mistresses and divorces. She and
her friends want to be married and have four well-spaced children, and not be bothered about politics and causes, those tire-
some concerns of their parents. Under the surface indifference,
Julia is warmhearted, responsive, innocently taking her privileges for granted; but she is capable of arrogant upper-class
attitudes expressed—to her own surprise sometimes—in her
mother's words. Usually she is quite at her ease with everybody. In the coffee bar where we see her first, she accepts an
invitation to sit down with her cup of coffee at a table with a
man who seems elderly to her but looks interesting. And so
begins an adventure with Jan Brod, a Central European exile,
resident in England, who had fought in the English army. He is
a writer, a Communist, and a Jew; and he is not at all sure that
he wants to return—if he can—to his country, which has had
political upheavals since he left. (Czechoslovakia fits the picture.) He would like on the whole to be naturalized. He has a
comfortable basement flat in North London in a house owned
by a pleasant German woman, Friedl, whose English husband
had been killed in the war, leaving her the house and some
money. She has a young daughter and a small son and likes
taking care of Jan Brod, who, as we—and Julia—eventually
learn, is the father of the little boy.

Of course Jan falls in love with Julia. Who wouldn't? His
love is whimsical, protective, and compassionate. He is amused
at her Englishness and her intellectual immaturity, and he is
often startled by her ignorance of all the problems that have
made up his experience and by her resentment that such problems exist. She sums up these problems as "politics," which she
hates. She seeks him out in his flat, types the manuscript of the
book he is writing, very competently does research for him,
spends some nights with him, makes friends with Friedl, tries
to get a better job for him through her father and to find him a

publisher, also through her father's influence. The scenes in which her father comes to town and they have lunch together are delightful. They are so careful not to interfere in any way with each other's lives. When she finally gains a horrified insight into the complexity of a refugee's life, she even tries to interest an important elderly personage in Roger's department to use his influence in Jan's naturalization case. This effort—over tea in the railroad station— is disastrous. Julia is learning all sorts of things about her own country which she had never dreamed of.

Jan's problems would be pretty dreary to read about, except for the fact that he has to explain them to Julia and to take care not to bore her or shock her into withdrawal. He is a writer and can tell a good story. Fellow refugees, and investigators into Jan's eligibility for naturalization, are always turning up in the flat, where Julia may be typing off in a corner, as his secretary; and what she overhears has to be explained afterwards. There is the matter of his first wife, for instance, whom he had married in a registry office abroad to save her from a concentration camp and to give her a chance to escape to England. He had never lived with her and had not seen her since. But, in answering questions in England, she tells a tale to please the officials of being ill-treated by her Communist husband. And there is Katie, another escapee. "When Katie went through the mill," explains Jan, "she simply burst into tears and said how the Communists had ill-treated her." "And had they?" asks Julia. "Actually not. But the Home Office have soft hearts, because Katie was naturalized almost at once. She wept on their shoulders. I know how Katie weeps. She used to be an actress in Budapest. Of course, knowing Katie, I wouldn't put anything past her." "Meaning what?" asks Julia coldly. "Meaning that she no doubt offered her services. One gets naturalized very easily if one does. She won't be much use to them because she's as stupid as a straw. . . ." Julia has stopped typing and is thinking, "I must get my father to explain all this. I don't understand a word of it." (237)[1]

Perhaps what puzzles Julia more than anything else is the wry pleasure Jan derives from contemplating the ways of the British authorities when faced with the ways of his Central European friends—and comparing the political traditions of the English with the passionate commitments and subtle ambiguities of Communists and ex-Communists. How can he, thinks Julia, find it sometimes so hilariously funny? When officials question him and his friends about a certain Miriam Hauptmann, who actually does not exist so far as they know, she becomes a joke to them and Jan even writes a poem about her, inventing her, and sends the poem to his brother in Czechoslovakia. Twelve of the stateless seeking citizenship get together and compare notes, fitting together the questions they had been asked, and there was nothing Miriam had not done. What a woman she must have been, they think. Julia asks if she was a spy, and he replies that she was a genius: "And not one of us had ever heard of her." Yet she is keeping them all in the limbo or statelessness. Julia thinks, "I must ring up my father and tell him I want to see him at once." (239-40)

The account of Jan's sessions with the two operatives from the government bureau, one who talks and one who is silent and dangerous, is pure comedy, but behind the comedy is frustration and suffering. Jan cannot help being an intellectual and dallying with definitions in attempting to answer their questions. But the Socratic method just doesn't work with security investigators. "Would you describe yourself as a stable personality?"—"Well in all honesty," he says, considering the question on its merits and from all angles, "I would describe myself as a well-integrated personality, but stable—no. That is going too far." Would he describe himself as an unpolitical character? "No, no, there is no such thing as an unpolitical person from Central Europe." But he is a nonpracticing politician, an artist. Is the book he is writing about politics? Well, yes, but from a humanistic viewpoint, and you will agree, he appeals to the questioner, as a good liberal democrat, that art has nothing to do with politics. Jan says this because "at the height of the cold war, there was not a respectable reviewer or critic in Britain who was not saying that art could have nothing to do with politics." (247-48) In the end Jan is refused, though he can reapply sometime. And in spite of his appreciation of the humorous aspects of the situation, he is very bitter, for he had always loved London because he loved Blake and Byron and

Dickens. And he decides to go back to his country, the way having been paved by his brother. So Julia is left to Roger.

How could this summer affair be carried on so easily? The answer throws light on what it could be like for such girls as Julia to live in the London of the 1950's. They could live in small flats, apart from their upper-class families, go about as they pleased, stay out nights, "take courses" if they wished, scrub the kitchen if they felt like it, and generally enjoy a freedom the mere idea of which would have appalled—or intoxicated—their grandmothers. That "room of one's own" of which Virginia Woolf wrote in the 1920's now offered far more than freedom to write novels. And this was London—relatively safe. Julia could, being lonely and unhappy, roam the streets all night, with no more risk than being questioned by a fatherly policeman at three in the morning on the Embankment. Julia's night stroll is a fascinating London tour, everything she experiences relating in some way to her emotional crisis. This is still Virginia Woolf's London, but postwar. Julia gets around more than any of Mrs. Woolf's heroines.

After Jan goes, in the weeks before Julia marries Roger—and she insists upon a full-dress church wedding—Julia reverts to the role of spoilt only daughter and plays it for all it is worth. Her parents are resigned, and Roger humors her. What would Jan have thought of her behavior? Waiting in the rain for a taxi, she thinks she will never be able to do anything again with an undivided mind, will always be seeing herself as Jan Brod would, and hating him. But he had said, "You're going to hate me, Julia." He had always understood everything about her; he took her seriously; Roger would never have the faintest idea of what she was like. Inside a taxi, with the rain slashing at the windows, she reflects how nice it is to wave at a taxi and be carried away comfortable and warm, and how Jan Brod would despise that. But what is the matter with comfort? Still she remembers how Jan had said that "something" might happen even in England, and she wishes it would. "I can't make a move out of all this for myself, but if something happened I would be pushed out . . . I'd understand it. I'd be part of it. Because of Jan Brod." He doesn't really despise her, but people like her are dead as far as he is concerned. "Are you quite sure we're

dead? . . . Are you quite sure that even in your half of the
world people want what you want, and not just comfort and
being able to get out of the rain?" The tears that fill her eyes
are of passionate regret. (333-34)

Mrs. Lessing told me in August, 1964, that she felt the characters she had created in this novel, especially Jan and Julia,
were wasted, because their possibilities were not fully developed. *Retreat to Innocence* is certainly not the well-integrated
work of art that we find in *The Grass Is Singing*. There are too
many threads in Jan's story, too many people involved, and too
many political complications in proportion to the central episode—the love story. The material calls for expansion into a
longer novel, or else compression into a novelette. But better
the wit and the comedy of some of the scenes in Jan's apartment than a neater and less amusing work of art.

II *Martha Quest*

Children of Violence is a series of five novels, of which three
have been published in England, a fourth is "work in progress,"
and a fifth is promised to complete the series. It was planned
and given its title when *Martha Quest* was published in 1952,
though the number of volumes was not stated. The second and
third in the series appeared in 1954 and 1958, respectively. Mrs.
Lessing is now returning to *Children of Violence*, after completing the remarkable—and very different—novel, *The Golden
Notebook*. The fourth volume, entitled *Landlocked*, covers the
years 1945-50. Only when the five are completed shall we be
able to judge the significance of the title, and to appraise her
success in developing her major theme, as stated in *Declaration:* "a study of the individual conscience in its relations with
the collective."

So far as one can tell from the first four novels, the individual
conscience belongs especially to Martha Quest, who is well
named but who is not seeking her own identity, that very popular quest of many contemporary fictional characters. Martha,
from her first appearance at the age of fifteen, has a well-
established identity—not fixed, of course; but one can count
upon it, through all the experiences she goes through in the
next dozen years, not to lose its main characteristics. A girl of

passionate vitality, eager for experience, chafing against restrictions, temperamentally rebellious: what was it like for such a girl, the daughter of English settlers, to grow up from a few years before World War II in Southern Rhodesia, a British colony, living first on a large farm and then in the capital city of the colony—Salisbury? And what was she rebelling against? Her family, of course, especially her mother's possessiveness; the patterns of a color-bar colonial society; the handicaps of her sex in the search for freedom and fulfillment. She is all through, at fifteen, with the education available to her, and all through with established religion. There are no restrictions on her reading, nor on her freedom to roam all over the half-wild veld country with a dog and a gun. It has already been pointed out that the fictional Martha Quest and her creator, Doris Lessing, grew up on the same farm; but we cannot properly carry the identification any further.

Just what Mrs. Lessing may have found at the little local station where the farmers went to ship their produce and to buy stores, she does not say. But Martha Quest found the Cohen boys, whose father kept a shop there; and Joss and Solly lent her books. Solly was in love with psychology and Joss with economics and sociology, and they talked things over when they had a chance. Here are Martha and Joss in one of their exchanges of ideas. *Joss:* You repudiate the color-bar? *Martha:* But of course. *Joss:* You dislike racial prejudice in all its forms, including anti-Semitism? *Martha:* Naturally. *Joss:* You are an atheist? *Martha:* You know I am. *Joss:* You believe in socialism? *Martha:* That goes without saying. Here Martha laughed, for she has a sense of humor, though it is not always working; but Joss frowned, for he could see "nothing ridiculous in a nineteen-year-old Jewish boy, sprung from an orthodox Jewish family, and an adolescent British girl, if possible even more conventionally bred, agreeing to these simple axioms in the back room of a veld store in a village filled with people to whom every word of this conversation would have the force of dangerous heresy."(53) [2]

Expressing such ideas to the Cohen boys scarcely prepared Martha for the shocked silence that greeted her at a party at the Van Rensbergs when her host drew her on to the thin ice of

British-Afrikaans relations, and she asked reasonably enough, "If you dislike us so much, why do you come to a British Colony?" Although as far as she was concerned, she added, he was welcome. His demand was that there should be rights for both languages, and she agreed, and added that she believed in "equal rights for all people, regardless of race." Whereupon her dancing partner hastily pulled her out to the veranda. The Cohen boys are important in Martha's later experience in Salisbury.

Martha Quest, A Proper Marriage, and *A Ripple from the Storm,* though closely linked, can be read as separate novels. The first ends with Martha's first marriage; the second, with the break-up of this marriage; and the third, with Martha facing not only the end of her second marriage but also the disillusionment of her first major involvement with "the collective." The narrative style is "straight, broad, direct"—the adjectives Doris Lessing uses in the preface to *African Stories* to describe the style of "The Pig," one of her earliest stories, in contrast to that of another early work, which is "intense, careful, mannered, self-conscious." These two styles she sees as the "two forks of a road"; she followed the first, it is obvious: a style "less beguiling" but a "highway to the kind of writing that has the freedom to develop as it likes." The last two volumes of the series will, one supposes, continue in the style of the earlier three. In the meantime Mrs. Lessing has written *The Golden Notebook* in quite a different narrative manner, one that plays tricks with chronology, for instance. But Martha's life flows on like a well-behaved river. The French have a name for this kind of novel—*le roman fleuve.* But in a discussion as brief as this must be, it will be best to keep firm hold on the theme of the series. Here is Martha, the individual conscience, and there is "the collective"; and how is the interrelationship explored?

Martha, coming to the capital from the veld to take a secretarial job in the law office of a Cohen relative, is full of ideas derived from books, and sees herself, as a girl, bound to suffer adolescence like a disease; as British, and therefore uneasy and defensive; as living in the 1930's, and so "inescapably beset with problems of race and class"; as female, and "therefore obliged to repudiate the shackled women of the past." She sometimes thinks unreasonably: if it has all been said, and we know it, "why do we have to go through the painful business of living it?" It is time to move on to something new. The epigraph prefixed to this part of *Martha Quest* is from Olive Schreiner: "I am so tired of it, and also tired of the future before it comes."

In the capital of the colony (which Mrs. Lessing calls Zambesia), she finds something new: a well-organized white colonial society, firmly based on the backs of African natives as servants in all capacities. Class divisions among the white population are not important, but the division into age groups is, and Martha is naturally drawn into the social activities of the young. The older people hold the financial, legal, and government positions; if retired, they are socially active. There are many more young men than girls in the town, and they fill positions in the Civil Service and the banks and the businesses. The men have their eyes out for any attractive new girls, and Martha is taken in charge first by Donovan Anderson, who is an only son and a mother's boy, and who would have made a dress designer of talent in a European capital. He is regarded with some derision in the social group, but is accepted, and he grooms Martha for entry into the group much as Shaw's Professor Higgins grooms Liza. The members of this group dine and dance at McGrath's Hotel, and they all belong to the Sports Club, of which the leading spirit is "Binkie" Maynard, a magistrate's son. His father is one of the most interesting characters in the series. The Sports Club could qualify as a "collective"; its members live a group life, very much in the public eye, very good examples of "togetherness." Anything—romances, quarrels—is permissible, if shared. Marriages tend to dissolve, and the partners to be reshuffled. Club children sleep in their prams through the "sundowners" and the dances, and grow up on the veranda among the hockey sticks, beer mugs, and bare legs, "like a doom made visible." It is like a never-ending fairy story, with everyone young, nothing threatened, Europe and politics a long way off. "It might be said that this club had come into existence, simply as a protest against everything Europe stood for. There were no divisions here, no barriers, or at least none that could be put into words; the most junior clerk from the railways, the youngest typist, were on Christian-name terms with their bosses, and mingled easily with the sons of Cabinet ministers; the harshest adjective in use was 'toffee-nosed,' which meant snobbish." (149)

Martha lives for weeks on the excitement of escape from the farm and her mother, and of initiation into this group; she sleeps too little, eats too little, drinks too much, as they all do, and is happily unaware that there are watchful critics among the social leaders—the Maynards, the Talbots, the Knowells, and so on. There is another little group in the town, serious thinkers, vaguely liberal and leftist, who get together to read and discuss, and she meets them through Joss Cohen before he goes to study law at a university. Two of them are Jewish girls, and one of them, Stella, is the wife of a Scotsman, Andrew. They become important in Martha's life later on. Her first love affair comes about indirectly through her anti-anti-Semitism, when she picks up a challenge at the club to be nice to "Dolly" King, who often plays in the band and is tolerated at the club. Identified as his girl, she persists in letting the affair run a course she tries to see as romantic, though she is dismally disappointed. Binkie and Donny and Stella disapprove, not because she has slept with "Dolly," but because "Dolly" is Jewish. After the affair is over, she is readmitted to their good graces.

Martha, subject to violent fluctuations of mood, is sometimes bored and confused and feels that life is escaping her; too many facts have been thrust at her, and she is too ignorant of the causes. On one early morning, oppressive with the atmosphere of a coming storm, she looks out of her window. A file of men and women is moving past; there is the soft padding of bare feet, and the ringing of boots on the tarmac. First come two policemen, buttons shining, hats cocked at an angle; then twenty black men and women, barefooted and shabby, handcuffed together. "It was these hands that caught Martha's attention: the working hands, clasped together by broad and gleaming steel, held carefully at waist level, steady against the natural movement of swinging arms—the tender dark flesh cautious against the bite of the metal. These people were being taken to the magistrate for being caught at night after curfew, or forgetting to carry one of the passes which were obligatory." In imagination she walked down the street as one of the file, feeling the oppression of the police state, and oppressed still more by the thought that it had all been described by Dickens, Tolstoy, Hugo, Dostoevsky. And all that terrible and noble indignation had achieved nothing; "the shout of anger from the nineteenth century might as well have been silent." Here came the file of prisoners, and on their faces "that same immemorial look of patient sardonic understanding." (176-77)

Ironically, it is her praiseworthy addiction to the liberal *New Statesman and Nation* that is her downfall. She happens to see a copy of the magazine on Douglas Knowell's office desk, and it is as if she recognized that they belonged to the same brotherhood. That gives her such a prejudice in favor of Douglas that, all the club members joyously cooperating, she is swept into a hasty marriage with this very proper, eligible young man. Magistrate Maynard watches the honeymoon couple drive off with another recently wedded pair, pursued by a riotous crowd of well-wishers from the club, who run down a native on the way, but shower him with silver as a recompense for his hurts. Maynard reflects sadly on the irresponsible younger generation that thinks it can do anything, if it can buy out of it afterwards. He has four more weddings to preside over; four more divorces, he reflects, in due time.

III   *A Proper Marriage*

At the end of *A Proper Marriage*, several years later, Martha, having left Douglas and her little daughter and her pleasant suburban home, is driving into town with her books and her suitcases to take up her life in another furnished room, when she is stopped by Mr. Maynard. "Deserting? . . . You look extraordinarily pleased about it." He is not going to forgive her for leaving her child, his goddaughter; but "I suppose with the French Revolution for a father and the Russian Revolution for a mother, you can very well dispense with a family." The divorce is not long delayed. The main interest of this volume is the story of how and why the proper marriage went on the rocks. This private drama is played out in the atmosphere of the war, and Mrs. Lessing's creation of that atmosphere is a brilliant achievement.

Even before the war actually began, the young people in the

capital of the colony, the newly-married Knowells among them, were dancing every night at the Sports Club, in the hotels, in halls, and in the courts of the hotels around braziers— for it was the African winter, with sharp, clear cold nights. "By midnight they were dancing as if they formed one soul . . . swallowed up in the sharp exquisite knowledge of loss and impending change that came over the seas and continents from Europe; and underneath it all a rising tide of excitement that was like a poison." (326) The young men were thinking of the moment when they could put on uniforms, "longing to be swallowed up in something bigger than themselves. . . . It was only necessary for the orchestra to play Tipperary or Keep the Home Fires Burning . . . for the entire gathering to become transformed into a congregation of self-dedicated worshippers of what their parents chose to remember of 1914." Though the authorities in Britain had not yet made up their minds how the colonies were to be used, one principle was decided: "the men from the Colonies were clearly all officer material, because of lives spent in ordering the black population about. The phrase used was: 'They are accustomed to positions of authority.'"

Sundowner parties are the occasion for gatherings of the best people, and Martha and Douglas are on the accepted list. The best people, old and young, form the group that Martha, by her hasty marriage, must establish relations with. The scene at one of these parties introduces characters we have not met, and the conversation throws light on the social, political, and racial attitudes of the society in this colonial government seat.[3] The big house is typical of the residences of the families accustomed to administer this and that part of the British Empire. The keynote is comfort, special adaptation to the climate: wide, shaded verandas, gardens, and plenty of native servants lodged in extensive native quarters back of the gardens.

Mr. Maynard likes to provoke Martha into expressing opinions, and on this occasion he points out the significance of some of the guests: Mr. Player, for instance, who "controls half the minerals in the central plateau" and can "hardly be expected to remain unmoved at the prospect of peace being maintained." Maynard, watching her because her face expresses so clearly what she is thinking about what she hears, gives her kindly advice: if she must feel so strongly, she had better learn to hide it. Colonel Brodeshaw, the host, has been saying, "If we conscript the blacks, the question of arming them arises." "Obviously not"—a unanimous murmur up and down the veranda; and Mrs. Maynard, a magisterial woman, expresses the general opinion: "If they learn to use arms, they can use them on us. In any case, this business of sending black troops overseas is extremely short-sighted; they are treated as equals in Britain, even by the women." Mr. Maynard comments to Martha that one of the advantages of living in the colonies is that there is an admirable frankness about politics; Mr. Player—who is the voice of Big Business—may talk about uplifting the masses of the people, but it is enlightened self-interest to realize that Africans cannot subsist healthily on mealiemeal and nothing else. Player knows that if the blacks are not to revolt, they must be fed and housed. Only recently, to say that was revolutionary. Martha is fascinated by the "smooth and savage" sentences in which Maynard expresses a cynical, disillusioned philosophy of history: the more things change, the more they remain the same. In the discussion about penal reform—prison or whipping for the natives—the opinions of the ladies range from Mrs. Maynard's "they don't mind prison—it's no disgrace to them" to gentle Mrs. Talbot's "the poor things shouldn't be whipped—everyone should be kind to everyone."

When war was declared, the first concern of authority was to explain through wireless and loud-speakers that it was the patriotic duty of the natives to join their white masters against the monster across the seas in a Europe they could scarcely form a picture of, "whose crimes consisted of invading other people's countries and forming a society based on the conception of a master race." Wartime Salisbury became an air-force training base, with, on its outskirts, camps of Nissen huts, hangars, runways, temporary houses, surrounded by fences of barbed wire —"as self-contained and isolated as those other towns outside the city, the native locations." Great numbers of young men came to be trained, from outside the colony and from Home— looking dwarfed and pallid instead of brown and well-fed, unwilling guests who noted the few amenities, which did not include women, but "with that calm commonsense which distinguishes the British workingman, decided to make themselves as comfortable as possible in circumstances fully as bad as they had expected."

Before long there was trouble because some of the innocent newcomers transgressed the color bar by bringing women (not, of course, black, but colored) into the bars, by offering black men cigarettes, even by talking and walking with them. This behavior was at first felt to be the result of ignorance, but there was something else—an atmosphere like "a persistent sardonic criticism," inarticulate and therefore unanswerable. As the trainees for the air force moved in, the young men of the colony moved out on trains to the north; first were the sons of fathers who had been able to afford their learning to fly. Scenes of farewell at the railway station integrate the individuals we know with the crowd.

After the first hectic days and weeks of the war, and even before Douglas joins up, Martha becomes preoccupied with the intimately personal business of having a baby. The little group she is now part of is that of the expectant mothers, and the scenes are in the office of the popular Dr. Stern and in the nursing home and in her own flat where she is visited by two of her friends in the same predicament, by her oversolicitous mother, and by her mother-in-law. This is a very introspective phase of Martha's life, her relations with the collective being in a state of suspension. The three young women discuss everything, resent their condition. They try to bring on miscarriages, consider abortion, and then become rather pleased with the prospect of motherhood. They continue the gay life of the club as long as they can.

One day Martha and Alice drove out in the rain to the veld and bathed in a muddy pool, very much interested in their own ungainly bodies and in the life of the pool. Martha saw a large snail "tilting through the grass stems, its pale brownish shell glistening and beautiful, the horned stalk of its head lifted high. Then, across the white-frosted surface of the pool, she saw an uncoiling in the wet mat of grass, and a lithe green snake moved its head this way and that, its small tongue flickering." (395) She didn't scream, she observed; she almost became the snake—like D. H. Lawrence, an adept at such identifications.

The business of having the baby in the nursing home is fully described. If one is interested in comparing literary fashions in novels separated by seventy years or so, one remembers Olive Schreiner's *Story of an African Farm,* whose heroine Lyndall asserted the right of women to question most of the late Victorian assumptions—sexual as well as religious, moral, and political. Lyndall was a precursor of the Martha Quests in the search for freedom. But her sex problems, including a baby, are veiled in a mist; they are strictly off stage. Martha's are set forth with clinical frankness; as vicarious experience, the account leaves little to be added. But because the whole nursing home episode is handled with the considerable humor that comes from Martha's alert response to people and things, the experience is— vicariously—quite enjoyable. To Martha, in her misery, the nurses seem indifferent. She comes out of a gulf of pain to see a young native woman scrubbing the floor; no one else is in the room. The woman smiles encouragement, lays her wet hand on Martha, says "Bad?" in her rich voice, and then croons an old nurse's song, "Let the baby come. Yes, missus, let it come." The moment the young pink nurse comes in, she hastily resumes her scrubbing. Martha later wants to see her baby, but her ward neighbor, already a day ahead of Martha, advises her, "You'd better do as they want, dear. It saves trouble. They've got their own ideas." (407) This section of the novel is introduced by a quotation from "How to Have a Baby": "You must remember that having a baby is a perfectly natural process."

Soon after the "natural process" is completed, Douglas is off to the war, and Martha is left in the flat with a lively baby, with the attentions of mother and mother-in-law, and with the occasional diversion of a date with an air force trainee, a situation almost certain to be misinterpreted, as Mr. Maynard points out to Martha, over whom he keeps a watchful eye. He likes to get through her defenses in argument, but he is especially intrigued by her failure to pay any tribute to "the authority he felt he enshrined." They go together to one of the meetings of the Contemporary Politics Discussion Circle, considered Leftist; Mr. Maynard has the idea that there are probably some able men in these vaguely socialistic clubs whom the government might make use of in the national emergency. Martha discovers that, for the first time in her life, she is sitting in a room with an African present as an equal—Mr. Matushi, who takes part respectfully in the discussion on education. So does Mr. Maynard, who had very recently fined him for not having a pass after nine o'clock. At the close of the meeting, Mr. Maynard suggests to him that he might be willing to represent his followers on a committee for raising funds; Mr. Matushi replies gently, "A person like myself, fined in the courts, might not be—acceptable?" And then he adds, with a "genuine bubbling amusement" which Martha, at this stage of her education, cannot understand, "Mr. Maynard, our people will do everything they can in this terrible war. They will fight well. It is only fifty years since we were honourably defeated by your soldiers. Our soldiers have already gone to fight with your soldiers against fascism for democracy." (458) On the way home with Martha, Mr. Maynard expresses his opinion about the need to create a middle class with special privileges among the Africans, but he adds that most of the whites are too stupefied to see the advantages of such a course. All these Africans can be bought—"they all overreach themselves if you give them time." Martha is hostile, but she feels herself as stupid as the majority of the whites. Her education, which was getting off to a good start, is halted by the return of Douglas, unfit for service because of ulcers but quite fit for a very well-paid administrative position, and able to purchase an attractive house in the suburbs. A couple of years will pass before Martha will again be concerned with politics.

Martha now found herself part of another well-defined group, the young married set living pleasant lives in an environment curiously like that of a suburb outside of New York or London—with the very important difference that there was no servant problem. Martha could play the housewife very comfortably with supervision over three or four "boys," a young nursemaid (black), and some useful little piccannins connected with the cook or the garden boy. Her cupboards were full, her husband had a car, and she passed her days, like her neighbors in the other pleasant houses, by going to tea-parties, gossiping about their servants, their doctors, and their children, and indulging in "daily orgies of shared complaint." They all had about the same income; houses partly paid for; furniture bought on "hire purchase," including refrigerators, washing machines, and electric stoves; and they went for holidays to the Cape once in four or five years ("getting off the altitude"). There were sundowner parties, dancing and cinema in town several times a week. "The great climax of their lives would come at fifty or fifty-five, when their houses, gardens, and furniture would be their own, and the pensions and policies bore fruit."

What began to worry Martha was the ease of her adaptation to this life; some instinct to conform must have dictated her entering this trap, "bound by a house and insurance policies until the gates of freedom opened at fifty." She was not even bored. "It was as if three parts of herself stood on one side, idle, and waited to be called into action." Oddly enough, the women talked a lot about economy, because all the mortgages and insurance policies and installment payments had to be kept going by ingenious ways of saving shillings on clothes and food; and so they were willing to "sink their youth," as Martha saw it, in acquiring multifarious small talents on the way to that great goal, a comfortable middle age. And if she yielded to the urge of her "female self" to have another baby, she instinctively knew she would be in the trap for good. She would end up like the middle-aged mothers of the young couples, dependent for emotional satisfaction upon the young people, and with nothing to do—left high and dry by this society. Martha had an obsessive fear of repetition. This obsession is humorously handled on one occasion when Douglas' widowed mother comes to see them; Martha is alert to a possible forecast of her own fate. For, if men were bound to marry their mothers, then she in the end would be like Douglas' mother; on the other hand, if she were doomed to become like her own mother—different as the two mothers were—then, "in its own malevolent way, Fate would adjust this incompatibility, too"—to her disadvantage.

Toward the end of this period of adapting herself to the special variety of suburban life that prevailed around her, the young air force officer of whom she had seen a good deal at the start of the war dropped in to see her. This is how the place looked to William: "Through the flowering hedges, beneath its sheltering trees, it looked very large, settled, permanent. The garden-boy was chatting with the nurse-girl under a tree, the piccannin was gathering peas in the vegetable bed, the house-boy was sweeping the deep flight of front steps. 'A delightful feudalism,' he remarked pleasantly. 'Truly delightful. And you the chatelaine of it all. . . . And I'll admit that there *are* worse ways of spending one's life.'" On leaving, he said: "If you ever feel like a nice change. . . ." (536) Restless and dissatisfied, she went into the house and began to read the newspapers—something she had neglected doing for some time, having become disgusted by their gloating tone over the invasion of Russia. But the situation had evidently changed. She rummaged in a cupboard and found a pile of dead newspapers. "Two years ago, the Russians had been dastardly and vicious criminals, plotting with Hitler to dominate the world. A year ago they were unfortunate victims of unscrupulous aggression, but unluckily so demoralized that as allies they were worse than useless. Now, however, they were a race of battling giants"—at a place called Stalingrad.

Two of the editorials were in a familiar tone: about "how the native population did not appreciate what the whites were sacrificing in uplifting them from their savage state, how they did not understand the dignity of labor, how they could not expect to be as civilized as the whites in under a thousand years, for this was the length of time it had required the British people to evolve from mud huts to democracy and plumbing." (537) Respected citizens warned not only of the agitators who were putting ideas into the heads of the natives but of the organizations spreading ideas inimical to white civilization—under cover of raising aid to Russia. And the advertisement columns gave notices of meetings by such organizations as "Help for our Allies," "Sympathizers of Russia," on subjects like "The Constitution of the Soviet Union," and "Life on a collective farm in the Ukraine." Martha realized that the group—some of the people she had known in town a couple of years ago—was at last "doing something," and she felt an excitement, followed almost immediately by boredom, for, if William and Jasmine or anyone else had been going among the people, like the heroes and heroines of an old Russian novel, there would have been much more noise in the press. "The colour-bar made that form of agitation impossible." But, when Douglas went off on a mission for some weeks, Martha went to town to look into these activities.

From this point on, there are two interwoven strands in the novel: Martha's renewed connection with a political "collective," leading on into situations forming the main interest of the next novel in the series, and the breakup of her marriage. We watch this marriage going on the rocks as if we were following the scenes and dialogue of a comedy on the stage; there is even a sort of chorus composed of the watching relatives and neighbors. Douglas more and more plays to the gallery. Martha characteristically withdraws and watches and questions; at the times when he is most emotional, her brain is ticking along with a cold analysis, trying to see things objectively, being reasonable ("Let's get this straight."), reminding him of facts, refusing to cooperate in making a scene. Accused of neglecting Caroline, she responds with the statistics of her day. The omniscient author, who cannot resist psychological explanation rather in the manner of George Eliot, points out a weakness in Martha's reasoning when she thinks, " 'I don't see how he can complain that I am what I always said I was.' For at the moment she forgot the years of feminine compliance, of charm, of conformity to what he wanted. They had all been a lie against her real nature, and therefore they had not existed." In short, she had as convenient a memory as Douglas.

As it became common knowledge that the Knowell marriage was not going well, the women of her set came to tell her in secret that they admired her courage and wished they could do the same—which, to them, meant simply escaping from an unsatisfactory marriage. It meant nothing to them that she wished to pursue a political interest against Douglas' wishes. She saw, too, that when a woman of her type, "who insisted on her rights to behave as a man would," was about to leave her husband, a whole automatic process was set in motion. The husband threatened to make her forcibly pregnant, accused her of infidelities, made self-abasing, weeping appeals difficult to withstand. And more frightening was the idea that they were in-volved in a pattern of behavior they could not alter. Douglas turned more and more from a sensible, responsible young man, within the limitations of his class, "though perhaps an angry one, into a sulky little boy, his lips quivering with self-pity."

Martha's father has given up the farm and taken a small sub-urban house. Mrs. Quest is anything but helpful, being rather on the side of Douglas. Martha goes to see her father, and the scene between them is one of the best. (Mrs. Lessing is singu-larly good with fathers and daughters.) Since much of the time he is withdrawn into his "inner world of memory and vague philosophical speculation," it is rather startling when he comes out of it and really looks at his daughter with his "shrewd and knowledgeable old eyes":

"What did you do it for?" he said suddenly, in a low reproachful voice. "It was so obvious it wouldn't be any good. You weren't even in love with him."

"Wasn't I?" she asked, surprised. She could not for the life of her remember what she had felt.

"You weren't in love with him, you've never been in love with anyone—anyone can tell it by looking at you," he said. That last sentence, cool, direct, the judgment of no less than an experienced man, caused her to look at him in respectful surprise. "I knew then it was a mistake—but no one can ever tell you anything. Can they now?" (528)

He advised her to think it over and not get herself in the family way again until she was certain whether she wanted to leave Douglas or not. In an embarrassed voice—it was years since they had openly shown each other affection—he said, "I'm very fond of you. . . ." Then he added that he had never liked that man, and didn't understand how she could have married such a "commercial traveller." They both paused to look at Caroline, engaged in pulling lilies off their stems: "the image of you at her age. Except for the eyes, of course. And the hair. Where did those eyes come from?" "Douglas' father, I believe," said Martha. What on earth did he mean? She was shocked by his reply: "Well, I've often wondered. . . . After all, you don't hold with our morals; as far as I can see there's nothing to prevent

Caroline being someone else's child." Did he think she had married under false pretenses? He couldn't see what would prevent her—and anyway there must have been some reason; perhaps she had been in the family way. And that she found extremely funny, because she had been, as a matter of fact (and as we know from earlier parts of the novel), and hadn't known it, though apparently everyone else had. Mr. Quest did not see the joke. "I think it's appalling," he said, taking comfort, however, in the thought that her generation was no more competent than his was. (529)

Martha's relationship with her father and with her mother, their relationship with each other, her relationship with Mr. Maynard, and with Douglas, and with Dr. Stern the baby specialist, and later with individual members of the political groups she becomes involved in: all of these relationships are handled with insight, often with humor and compassion, and with a technique that makes full use of dramatic situation and dialogue. Such good use, in fact, that the omniscient author does not need to explain as much as she does or to indulge in pertinent general reflections that are not so much obvious as unnecessary. They are often very interesting, nevertheless.

In a final scene with the hysterical Douglas, when he threatened to shoot Martha and Caroline, Martha went out in the moonlight to take refuge with her mother, and had the door slammed in her face. Douglas really enjoyed playing his role in this melodrama, and Martha, though frightened, was disgusted. She sought advice in town from her old friend Jasmine Cohen, who first listened to a long self-critical speech about how "intellectuals were doomed to futility because they always thought about things instead of doing them." Then she said, "Why don't you leave? There might be a revolutionary situation at any moment, and here you are wasting time on personal matters." The voice of the collective.

IV   A Ripple from the Storm

Martha, back in town, found the "Help for our Allies" committee busy raising medical supplies for Russia and a "Sympathizers of Russia" proposing that the two groups join in celebrating the anniversary of the November Revolution. At this moment even the respectable pillars of society felt it might be possible to celebrate the Revolution because of the heroism of Stalingrad. Martha moved into another furnished room, secured a small job, and plunged into committee work. The gossip was that she had left Douglas for William who was still in the air force training camp; Douglas, who liked to believe that, threatened to have him cited as corespondent; and William believed Douglas was using his influence to have him "posted" and rather enjoyed the prospect of a legal fight. That reaction finished William for Martha. A fight over the possession of her! She saw the two men as one, "identical with the pompous, hypocritical, and essentially male fabric of society." Dismayed at the view the town gossip took of her, she simply put out of her mind the people who had made up her life a short time before, lived in the "group," and felt as if she were invisible to anyone but the group.

The air force training camp furnished an odd assortment of interested young men who took part in the meetings, worked on committees, and made love to the girls. (*Martha:* Murdoch has just proposed to me. *Jasmine:* Well, he proposed to me last week. And he proposed to Marjorie the day before yesterday and went and got drunk when she said she was going to marry Colin. *Martha:* They're all mad. That means that all the R.A.F. members have proposed to us all in the last month.)

Then there were a few refugees from Europe, especially the German Communist, Anton Hesse, whom Martha had met in her earlier town activities, a thin, fair man of thirty, with keen blue eyes "of the kind which look as if there is white ice behind the iris." He had escaped—we are told by the author—from Hitler's Germany to England, had adjusted to life there only to be sent away to this colony, where he had spent three years "of such boredom and despair he had considered suicide. But communists do not commit suicide"—a principle he clung to like a raft in the black sea of despair. He loathed "the empty, illeducated, easy-going Colonials; he despised the life of sundowners and good times . . . Above all, the political backwardness of the place depressed him." He dreamed of the moment when he could go back to Germany, but his comrades and his wife were dead. He spent his time reading Marxist classics and studying Russian: "a man in cold storage for the future." He was not at all eager to start work again in this half-baked country with a group of romantic amateurs, and he felt a deep reluctance to come out of his shell and "start feeling again." But—he said to himself—a Communist has the duty to work in whatever country he finds himself. So he began to work again, and made himself known to another Party member, a Scotch corporal at the camp, Andrew McGrew.

These two Communists surveyed the prospects for forming a Communist group: a dozen men in the air force, who were not allowed to take part in politics, a handful of aliens and refugees, a few girls who wanted love affairs and a little excitement —scarcely the basis for a group. And besides, "the working people of this country are black." McGrew, who respected Hesse, knew of his underground work and torture in prison; but he did not find him "the sort of chap I'd like to spend an evening in the pub with." There were undercurrents of antagonism between them, which unpolitical members of a committee felt but didn't understand. Martha soon learned that "the shortest acquaintance with politics should be enough to teach anyone that to listen to the words people use is the longest way around to an understanding of what is going on." (*A Ripple from the Storm*, 13)

Martha was a most earnest worker on committees; as soon as the Communists began to put some sort of order into the meetings, she had definite, assigned tasks. Again, as in the days before her marriage when she was caught up in the social whirl of the Sports Club, she was not eating enough or sleeping enough, and she neglected her health to do her political duty at any cost. The result was that she fell seriously ill in her furnished room. In one of her feverish nightmares she dreamed of the half-fossilized, extinct creature already referred to as a kind of symbol of the African question. Members of the group were much more helpful than her neurotic landlady, and Anton Hesse proved to be a kind and efficient nurse, taking the responsibility of calling in the doctor, and being so gentle and understanding that she said to herself, "Suddenly he's human." And though he was very fatherly and brotherly, she was half excited and half panic-stricken at the thought he might be falling in love with her. Jimmy Jones, an English working-class boy in training at the camp, competed with Anton in the role of nurse; but he could not resist the opportunity of instructing her in proper working-class attitudes and criticizing her bourgeois behavior: "When I see you bourgeois girls I think of my mother and what she had to take from life, and believe you me you could learn a thing or two from her." To which, with growing exasperation, Martha retorted, "All of you working-class men have this damned sentimental thing about your mothers." Angry, Jimmy said, "My mother was the salt of the earth. My dad died when I was ten and she brought me up and my two sisters on what she got by cleaning offices." "Good, then let's arrange things so that women have to work eighteen hours a day and die at fifty, worn out, so that you can go on being sentimental about us." (111-12)

Jimmy is a very interesting study, with his deadly seriousness, his naïveté, his devotion to the causes he is determined to understand and promote. He all but breaks up some of the committee meetings, and he certainly makes them far more entertaining than they would otherwise be. His share in the proceedings contributes to comedy effects, and we need them. For are there any fictional subjects more dead than old political situations and defunct committees?

At one of the meetings where the comrades were engaging in self-and-group-criticism, Jimmy raised the question of lipstick, red nails, and fashion magazines: that was not "communist"; women should be respected and not behave like—but he couldn't bring himself to say like what. Anton, chairing the meeting, was not amused and reminded them that this was not a music hall. "May I suggest that we appoint an evening for the discussion of the position of women?" But they would not stop. Jasmine called Jimmy's attitude very sectarian; if a majority vote decided that women comrades must give up cosmetics, she would regard it as masculine domination; all men, Communists or not, had remnants of middle-class ideas about women. Martha made some humorous remark that upset another working-class lad who had been trying to educate himself by reading *War and Peace*. He had discovered from reading "this Count Tolstoy" that Comrade Matty's manner was middle-class; the middle class say things that are serious in an unserious way; that is contemptuous—one has to think, do they mean it or don't they?

These two lads are not the only ones who trouble the proceedings. There is Maisie, who has joined the group through marriage with Andrew McGrew; she is simple and devastatingly honest and, like Jimmy, wants to get things straight. The small policy-making inner group is expected to study a 150-page document prepared by the Communist leaders, about how the colony should be run if the Communists should take power; an admirable document, it is voted upon clause by clause and accepted. The meeting feels quite contented with itself until Maisie rises to speak: "What I want to know is this. I mean to say, what's the point? You—I mean we, aren't even standing for elections, so there's no chance of putting any of it into practice. And Andrew explained to me yesterday about there's no revolutionary situation now, so you aren't thinking of being in power at all. So why go to all this trouble?" Anton: "But Comrade Maisie, it is our responsibility to put forward a policy so that the people will know where we stand." Maisie: "But you're a secret group, so they can't know, can they?" (207)

Here a new recruit from among the refugees, a Greek who had been fighting in the mountains under Communist leadership, came to the rescue of the leaders, speaking directly to Maisie—he never made general speeches: "We may be only a few here. But we are more than just a few people. We are the communist ideal. . . . And if two communists find themselves somewhere—let us say suddenly in a strange town, they know they are not just two people, but that they are communism. And they must behave with self-respect because they represent the idea." Even if one man is alone in prison, "he is a communist, and therefore not alone." This Greek never loses sight of the human individual; we must, he says, try and live like Socialists who care for each other and for people. He had been pleased with the group when it had helped Maisie solve a very personal problem and had brought about her marriage. For the light it throws on the community as well as upon the group, this affair of Maisie's deserves notice. It is a little comedy, and it brings Mr. Maynard back into the picture.

We had last seen Maisie—a friend of Martha's from the early days in town—with a group of women at the railroad station bidding farewell to their husbands, off to the war. Maisie's husband, her second, was killed. Before Binkie Maynard in his turn went into the service, Maisie and Binkie became lovers. Little as class distinctions counted in Salisbury, Maisie was yet definitely outside the magistrate's circle, and, when she found herself pregnant and approached Maynard on the subject of marriage, his first thought was to buy her off or to pay for an abortion in Johannesburg. He let her think that "compassionate leave" for Binkie to come back and marry her could not be obtained. This was not true. The Maynards simply did not want Maisie as a daughter-in-law.

Maynard encountered in Maisie a type of girl he did not understand, one with her own standards. She explained that she and Binkie were "engaged" and so they took precautions; but with her two husbands, she had wanted a baby; they had done nothing, but she didn't get pregnant. "Well, that's life," she ended humorously, with the tears running down her face. The conversation went on until Maisie realized with indignation what Mr. Maynard was thinking—that she was trying to put something over on him. "You needn't think that I don't know why you asked me not to marry Binkie on his leave. You think I'm not good enough. . . . I don't like the way you think. . . . I like Binkie well enough, he's a fine kid, but you're too much for me."

Maynard was uncomfortable. He realized she wasn't any good at blackmail—if that was what she was trying; and he was even rather unhappy because he had a sort of yearning for a granddaughter. Right after this conversation, Maisie met Martha on the street, remembered that Martha was reputed to be a Red, and that Reds believed in free love, and told Martha her troubles—and that she wanted the baby but couldn't have it. Martha characteristically remarked that it was disgraceful women couldn't have babies if they wanted to, husbands or not. But Maisie was no rebellious feminist; she knew a girl who had a baby without a husband and everyone treated her like dirt. Thereupon Martha came down from the region of principle to examine the problem in hand. Maisie didn't want to marry Binkie, if she had to have types like Maynard in her life. "I'd like to have the baby, Matty. I've had the three boys—my two husbands and Binkie, and I wish I could have a baby to myself." (120-24)

Maisie's problem finally became the group's, and discussions about it replaced in the meetings theoretical Marxism. How it came about that she married one of the Communists is one of the funniest and, in its way, most touching episodes in the book —one of the ripples in the storm.

Talking with Maisie, Martha had called Maynard a "damned old reactionary," but he continued to educate her in the ways of the world outside the group, talking to her as an equal—that is, as one white person to another. He advised her and the group, whose activities were beginning to worry him, to leave the Kaffirs alone; what did she suppose they were going to change? "We happen to be in power, so we use power." History to him was a record of misery, brutality, and stupidity; always knaves administer fools. If, for reasons he failed to understand, the processes of government interested her, let her play her cards right and get into a position where she had power; marry a politician and run him; or, if she wanted to do the dirty work herself, then become a town councilor, and eventually. . . . Realizing that Martha was looking at him as if he were a "specimen of horror from a dead epoch," he concluded that she should remember this isn't Britain, which makes allowances for social adolescents. "This country's a powder-keg and you know it. The whole thing can go up at any moment—and if you imagine that a horde of savages wouldn't cut your throat as well as mine, then you're a fool." (57-58)

From this "nightmare of recurring and fated evil" that had the power to haunt Martha, she was sometimes rescued by the spirit of hope pervading the happier meetings of the group—as when Anton quoted the words of the great men of his faith and held his audience spellbound with the vision of men making their own history, cutting away the ugly past: "Comrades, this is the dawn of human history." The calm voice linked her "with those parts of her childhood she still owned, the moments of experience which seemed to her enduring and true; the moments of illumination and belief." She felt an influx of strength,

as when the Cohen boys at the station had put books in her
hands, as if giving her a key. (65-66)

The group was at this time drawn into cooperation with the
committees of other political dissidents. The atmosphere was a
little like that of United Fronts in other parts of the Western
world. There was a Social Democratic Party, which had seven
members of Parliament and was the official opposition to the
Government. Mrs. Van der Bylt was the party's secretary, a
town councilor, and an active worker in welfare organizations.
A very full account is given of her and of her husband, a barris-
ter, both of them members of an old Cape family, Dutch by
origin. Before her marriage, she had been taken to England
and Switzerland to broaden her mind, and on the voyage she
had read Olive Schreiner's *Story of an African Farm,* which had
started an intellectual revolution in her. A very sensible girl, she
soon realized that her development "must depend on her own
efforts and that they must be secret efforts." She behaved very
properly as wife and mother but, reading Socialist and suffra-
gette writings behind locked doors, she became an atheist, a
Socialist, and a believer in racial equality.

A surprise to Martha was the appearance, at the first execu-
tive meeting of Mrs. Van's party which she attended, of her
girlhood acquaintance, the Scotsman Mr. McFarline—here described so that any reader of *The Antheap* could immediately
identify him: "He was chanting the classic phrases of the socialist credo with every appearance of passionate belief." Martha
was stunned, in spite of being prepared for evidences of hypoc-
risy in the party. (The trade unionists that represented labor in
the party "used the slogans of socialism in defense of their own
position, which was to protect their living standards against the
black workers.") Mr. Playfair, the Big Business man, was present, too, and the seven members of Parliament. Martha's education proceeded very fast as she listened to the discussion of
certain plans of action. Obviously, she and her five comrades
were there "as pawns in some internal battle they did not yet
understand." (189-90)

What that battle was about is recounted with the zest Mrs.
Lessing shows for political manoeuvres. There will be developments arising out of these episodes and these actors later in the

series—of that the reader is confident. Just after this new phase of Martha's political activity commenced and the atmosphere in the capital became more and more disturbed, Martha had to decide whether or not to marry Anton. But the C.I.D. informally called upon Anton's employer and told him that Anton, an enemy alien, was known to be having an affair with a British woman and that such relationships were frowned upon. And it had been known to happen in the past that enemy aliens, misconducting themselves, were returned to the internment camp. The matter was conducted in the great British tradition: "no one had actually threatened anyone, or brought any direct pressure to bear"; everybody was very uncomfortable; but the effect was that Anton had better toe the line. Marriage would retrieve the situation. Here was Anton, antifascist and anti-Hitler and yet treated like an enemy. He left the decision to Martha—no easy decision. The whole episode of the marriage —everybody being drawn in somehow—is both sad and funny.

At intervals in the narrative, this or that African appears briefly, and at one political meeting in connection with a local election, a group of them has been invited to attend, though not of course to participate actively. They are permitted to speak of the injustices they suffer. Mrs. Van interrupts an old African schoolteacher to point out that there is not a single African woman present, and the feminists take over in a lively interlude during which one of them proclaims, "Men! if there's one thing that teaches me there's no such thing as colour [it] is that men are men, black and white."

The activities that Mr. Maynard warned Martha against were among the Colored population, rather than the Black; and members of the group, including the air force boys (in civilian clothes), took turns selling the *Watchdog* (a Left propaganda sheet published in South Africa) in the Colored quarter, where whites were permitted to go. True, the few thousand Colored in the town were economically and politically unimportant, and in principle the group should work among the Africans, the true proletariat; but the Coloreds were at least physically accessible. That stubborn lad Jimmy Jones found these working people in the quarter easy to understand, and he tried to do more than sell them papers; he wanted to help them in personal problems of illness and so on. Anton's disapproval of this irrelevant humanitarianism made Jimmy even more stubborn; good relations with people were more important to him than theories drawn from an analysis of the class forces. Much troubled by the complexities of his new political life, Jimmy sneaked out of the camp one night to find and talk with an African, Elias, the official interpreter in the magistrate's court and the unofficial spy in attendance at group meetings. Jimmy did not know that, of course; he liked Elias. Cutting across country, the city boy breathed in the fresh, tart air of the high veld, looked at the immense sky, smelt the grass, and thought of sleeping out in the moonlight, until near the swampy river banks he discovered that the dark objects on his legs were large horny beetle-insects, and went into a tantrum of fear and disgust. A vividly realized night journey in a fearsome land!

Coming to a cluster of native huts and hearing a banjo, he knocked, only to find the African scared to death of this white soldier abroad after midnight. He had better luck in another settlement, where half a dozen young men, with mouth organs, banjo, guitar, and drums, quietly playing, welcomed him and continued to play softly, "because this was long after hours, long after the time when regulations said lights out, no more music, sleep now so that you will be fresh for the white man's work in the morning." Drums had beaten through the childhood of all these dark boys, city boys now, but bred in the villages of a country "where drums were seldom silent." Here in this room were both the hide-covered native drums and drums bought secondhand from the white man's band, and sometimes "the two kinds of drums spoke together, against each other, as if talking each other out in argument." "Sometimes, because of the necessity for caution and secrecy, a soft music came into life, that sang and questioned and hesitated, music born out of secrecy, double-talk, and the brotherhood of oppression."

There was little for Jimmy to do there. Then he found Elias' hut. He was not welcome at three in the morning, if at any time, and especially unwelcome when he said he wanted to talk about the future, and Socialist plans, and how "we can work to deliver your people from bondage . . . we must help each other, comrade!" Elias wailed with fear: "Go now, baas, please go now!" Jimmy went and ended up in the Colored quarter at the house of a woman whose sick son he and the group had been interested in.

Elias reported to Maynard, and Jimmy's half-mad adventure in brotherhood ended in the posting of himself and two other air force boys. Maynard did not take Elias' frightened tale very seriously, but he told his wife that she had better give the names Elias had mentioned to her cousin to the Air Force Administration. This is one of the best episodes in the book, drawing together threads in the longer narrative to make a meaningful pattern.[4]

The end of A Ripple from the Storm finds Martha and Anton increasingly at odds politically and personally. In spite of many moments of elation and belief, Martha cannot believe that Socialism will cure everything. What about the difficulties of "re-educating the older generation to socialist ethics"—a question Martha and Jasmine, out of their experience, often debate together. Arguing with Anton, Martha had said, "I sometimes think a good deal more than socialism is needed to cure this place." And now the group is broken up. There are only three Communists left. The political opposition is fragmented into the Social Democratic Party, which gives some tokens of good will to Africans, and the newborn Labour Party, which represents White Labour. The closing dialogue ends on a note of futility:

Anton: "The development in this country accurately reflects the same development in the Union of South Africa, and it is proof of the necessity for a communist party."

Martha: "But, Anton, there are only three of us left." Two clear convictions existed in her mind: everything inevitably had happened in the way it had happened; no one could have behaved differently; and everything that had happened was "unreal, grotesque, and irrelevant."

Anton: "Yes, yes, but that is because of the objective political situation. We must make a fresh analysis of the position and begin again."

She was overwhelmed with futility.

V *Landlocked*

Landlocked is the fourth volume in the series *Children of Violence*. The comments that follow are based on a reading of Mrs. Lessing's unrevised typescript. When the series is complete, with a fifth volume, *Landlocked* will be published with *A Ripple from the Storm* in one volume (Simon & Schuster edition).

A Ripple from the Storm closed on the note of futility. Martha's relations with the political group and her marriage with Anton, the dedicated Marxist leader, form a pattern of disillusionment in spite of moments of enthusiasm and enlightenment. The epigraph that precedes the opening chapter of *Landlocked* suggests a possible theme for the next stage of Martha's development:

> The Mulla walked into a shop one day.
> The owner came forward to serve him.
> "First things first," said Nasrudin,
> "did you see me walk into your shop?"
> "Of course."
> "Have you ever seen me before?"
> "Never in my life."
> "Then how do you know it is *me?*"

How does Martha know she is Martha?

The war is not yet over when we pick up Martha's story in the colonial capital. She is twenty-four, still married to Anton, still secretary to a lawyer; her father is chronically ill and her mother confined to nursing him; her little girl Caroline lives with Martha's ex-husband Douglas and his new wife, but often visits Mrs. Quest, although not when Martha is there; Caroline is taught to call her mother "Aunt Mattie." The first pages of the novel gather up the strands of Martha's life and reintroduce us to the people we have already met. Other characters come on the scene later. Maisie, divorced, lives over the restaurant where she works as a barmaid, with her little girl Rita; and the Maynards hover around, hoping in one way or another to rescue Rita, their son Binkie's illegitimate child, from what they consider a sordid future with Maisie. Their manoeuvres provide comedy. The Cohen boys, Joss and Solly, now out of the army, are pursuing Trotskyist and Stalinist paths, respectively. Athen, the Greek resistance fighter, still in training as a pilot, is hoping to be sent to Greece. He is the conscience of those who are left in the group, still the convinced Communist, but caring less for theories than for human values; destined to die in a Greek prison, and destined to remain for Maisie her hero, though he has often made her resentful precisely because of his goodness. There is some obscure plotting going on involving Africans, who have a center for contact in the home of the sick Johnny Lindsay, an old miner, born in Cornwall, a veteran of labor troubles in the Rand. He lives in sin with the blowsy, middle-aged, goodhearted Flora. Johnny is most exceptional in this color-bar society in that he has always disregarded the bar and oddly enough has got away with it. So it is in his house that black and white can meet.

The people that gather in his sickroom are an odd lot. Jack Dobie is a Red political agitator from the Clyde. Mrs. Van der Bylt, Dutch Socialist from the Cape, we have already met. And Martha herself, English, is married to a German-Jewish refugee and is mistress to a Polish peasant—Thomas Stern. (But of that affair, later.) The Africans from various places—Nyasaland, Northern Rhodesia, Portuguese territories—are beginning to wake up. Officially they are allied with the Social Democratic party, but that party is split into Reds, Kaffir "lovers," and white trade unionists; and the Conservative party runs the government. Mrs. Van der Bylt wishes to develop self-confidence in the blacks by a course of study in the edifying history of certain white nations—with the idea that the blacks will see that they themselves couldn't be any more stupid. But Mr. Matushi, one of the Africans, wants to study revolutionary tactics and to learn how to get rid of white governments. Johnny Lindsay, who has in his head the history of the Rand and the old struggles prior to 1914, tries to tell the story for the benefit of the blacks, who listen to these tales of the white men's labor troubles. Martha takes notes, to preserve this living record. Russia—for years the ideal—is talked about now in terms of "contradictions"; this is a code word, standing for everything the Soviets do which contradicts what might have been expected of them in their Socialist aspect.

Martha still dreams, and the dreams suggest her psychological state. The recurrent dream of the moment is of a house with many different rooms. Sometimes the house sinks into decay like the ruined house on the high veld—"collapsed into a mess of ant-tunnelled mud, ant-consumed grass"—this home which had been "the small shelter for the English family that they had built between teeming earth and brazen African sky." Martha is trying at this time to keep "separate" and hold at bay what is best in herself, walking "like a housekeeper in and out of different rooms, but the people in the rooms could not meet each other or understand each other." When she is talking politics with the Cohen boys, or discussing Maisie's problems—in whatever group she may be—the idea of a central lighted space in the house of many rooms takes shape. Emotions come and go like actors, but she herself is a spectator. The house of rooms is an image of the disparate elements in Martha's life and personality. She is waiting. She, like the little colonial community when the war ends, is landlocked.

Inescapable in the background is Martha's family problem: the dying father, the relationship full of antagonism with her mother, the separation from Caroline. Though Mrs. Quest tries to keep Martha from seeing Caroline, Martha inadvertently witnesses a scene between the dying old man and the child—the old man clutching at youth—that revolts her, and also makes her wonder what she had meant five years ago when she thought she was setting Caroline free. At one period before her father dies, Martha often walks the streets of the town at night after curfew, thinking of the chance by which for five years of her life she had been living in this little unharmed city, most of the time bored, waiting for life to start, while forty-four million human beings had been murdered by their kind. In imagination she argues over the problem of violence with her lover Thomas Stern, who has gone to fight in Israel. Once she stands outside her parents' lighted bedroom window and watches their shadows on the blind: "The house was more than ever like a nightmare. All her most private nightmares were made tangible there; and that is why she stood outside it at night, looking at it like a stranger." Her dreams during this period are of a high, dry place of drought, and she longs for the sea.

She is somewhat freed from the pressure of the family problem by the return from service of her brother and the beneficial effect this has on Mrs. Quest and even on the dying father. The brother marries and moves out into the country on a farm; the old man dies; what is Mrs. Quest to do? After a lifetime of nursing, she is deprived of her role of victim: "The essence of Mrs. Quest was that she could never be censored for anything —she was so much a victim. . . . The defeated one in the right. The old, the exploited, the miserable, are to be pardoned. . . . For years and years now, Mrs. Quest had not been allowed to be more than a physical being. And now, suddenly, there was nothing for her to do. . . . Mrs. Quest would suddenly find herself on her feet—her physical memory had told her legs that it was time for her husband's wash or his medicine." How was she to use all her knowledge, her energy? How deal with "the sudden explosion of old needs, which was bound to make itself felt, now when at last the braces were taken off Mrs. Quest's real nature—which was gay, kind and sociable?" Realizing that Martha is thinking of going to England—if she can secure a divorce—Mrs. Quest gives her a bunch of old keys to boxes and trunks, left behind in England. Pathetic little hints show all too clearly that Mrs. Quest wants to have Martha take her to England, to share her life there. Nothing could more terrify Martha —the reader does not need to be told that. Martha can only counter these hints by the evasion "but I have not gone yet." In the end Mrs. Quest goes to live with her son, to face the final frustration of an unwanted mother-in-law.

Martha Quest's parents, from start to finish, are triumphs of characterization, marked by probing insight, grim humor, and profound compassion.

The relationship with her family is one of the rooms in that house of Martha's recurrent dream. Another is the room of her marriage with Anton, which has subsided into a kind of friendly equilibrium, with the question of divorce in suspense —more waiting. Anton suffers over the end of the war, over what is happening in defeated Germany. He tries to reach people he had known before his exile; he is not sure whether he can become or desires to be a naturalized British citizen. The old Germany which would have killed him is dead; from the new Germany, he gets no answer to his letters. Finally he receives his British citizenship, but the divorce hangs fire. The confused emotional state of the exiles is revealed effectively during a scene in the local cinema, when the audience watches a news reel of wretched German soldiers limping across a war-torn countryside, to the accompaniment of jeering comments by the commentator. The sight arouses uneasy compassion in the audience, but Thomas Stern, who has just heard from a friend horrifying details of murder camps, resents the compassion.

Martha's love affair with Stern is another room. The actual room over the barn at his brother's farm, where they meet for afternoon love-making, is for many weeks or months her "center." She loves Stern as she certainly never loved either Douglas or Anton. This Polish-Jewish peasant, who has a wife, the daughter of an exiled Polish professor, and a child, living on a farm not far from the capital, is the most enigmatic and unpredictable of Martha's lovers. His going to Israel to fight is the outlet of his need to repay with violence the violence of which he had been the victim during his war service. When he returns, he is changed in a way Martha cannot understand. She is haunted by a vivid dream that he is about to be hanged. He takes up new work on the railways that brings him in contact with African workers, and he makes reports about hygiene and working conditions to a Foundation. When he dies suddenly of blackwater fever, Martha has to go over these reports left in his hut—a confused mélange of biographical notes, personal memories, and native anthropological material, out of which she can make nothing coherent enough to send to the Foundation. She is left with the riddle of personality: in what ways is the person revealed in these documents the one she had known so intimately? ("How do you know it is me?") Thinking over his death, of which she had heard the same night her father died, she feels that Thomas had chosen to die: "He had gone out to die, had made a death for himself, and so he had restored dignity to human beings who choose more often to be animals."

During these months and years after the end of the war, there are ripples from the storms outside the colony. Members of the "group"—"that pathetic little organism"—feel the change in the political atmosphere when they try to hold meetings. There is no longer tolerance of the "Reds," as there was while the outcome of the war was in doubt. A disturbing book appears written by a defecting Russian; if what it says is true, everything Martha has believed for the past seven years is a lie. A meeting to discuss the book fizzles out. Among the Africans and the "contacts," a confused shift of power and politics is going on. "One evening the radio remarked in the unemphatic almost affable voice which unfolds history in our bloody times" that there was going to be a strike. The white citizens become hysterical and begin to berate their black servants, who do not know what it is all about, but become apprehensive; many of them run off to the veld to sit it out, whatever it is. The strike, beginning on the railroads, was to spread to the farms. (Not only was there no right to strike, but no right to form unions among the Africans.) The strike is about the only action in *Landlocked,* and we follow its course only as it affects the white population in the town.

Martha joins the two formidable matrons, Mrs. Maynard and Mrs. Van der Bylt, to consult over what is to be done. Pickets, hitherto unknown agents of strike activity, have appeared to herd domestic servants into the locations, where they go bewildered and reluctant; after four or five days they begin to suffer from food shortages. They are really shut up because the authorities are afraid of what the militant whites—with a vigilante psychology—might do. Soon not an African is to be seen, and the white ladies have to do domestic work to which they are totally unaccustomed. The strike degenerates into absurdity. Old Johnny Lindsay dies in the midst of the confusion, and Martha and Mrs. Van work with the papers and notes he has left, finding themselves often in disagreement—the rift in the attitudes of old Socialist and young Communist. Mrs. Van, a strict moralist, cannot take Flora in her stride; nor can she understand the fierce joy in life which made old Johnny feel zest even in the cruelties of past conflicts. Martha seems to play the role, temporarily, of recorder of events and people otherwise sure to be lost in the currents of history. Perhaps at a later stage in the chronicle we shall learn what she makes of it all—for she takes Stern's strange records with her to England.

Landlocked ends with a political meeting that plays up the swift changes in public attitudes, and the bewildering rapidity with which one political generation succeeds another. But there is recurrence in the midst of change. Martha and her old friends Marjorie and Jasmine—all of them barely thirty years old—are suddenly the Old Guard; they are patronizingly invited by new agitators, ten years their junior, to attend a discussion on present affairs. An impassioned young orator holds the meeting spellbound with what are to Martha the familiar dreams of wide networks of agitation and of sums of money about to materialize out of the blue. (There are no Africans present.) She thinks he will have his way with the audience, will set things in motion, and in what he shapes will be the seeds of its own destruction. "So you can foretell the end of what you are creating now, if you know how to look for the signs." If only this or that condition is present, the vision may be realized; but the disillusioned Martha, at twenty-nine, reflects that it never is—remembering the "dead days eight years ago." This meeting, proclaims the orator, echoing Lenin, is called to "establish socialism in this country, now." And who will establish it? Who are the "we" of the orator? Martha and Jasmine ask this question. An Indian in the audience requests that someone sum up the world situation; the speaker, referring to his notes, launches into "an analysis of the situation"; and Martha reflects: "Not a patch on Anton in his heyday." The topic for general discussion is announced: what contribution will the newly created Communist China make to the world order? Oddly enough, after several hours of talk, there is unanimity about this contribution. Jasmine, politely invited to sum up, declares that Communist China will "restore to communism moderation, calm, sense, humanity, humor, tolerance."

One can only say (in 1964) that the political ironies have deepened in this volume of *Children of Violence.*

CHAPTER 5

The Golden Notebook

I *Each His Own Wilderness*

IN *Each His Own Wilderness,* produced at the Royal Court
Theatre in 1958, there are interesting foreshadowings of
characters and situations in *The Golden Notebook,* and of the
feminist theme of "free women." Two middle-aged women,
Myra and Milly, widowed or divorced, each have a son whom
she has brought up, Tony and Sandy, respectively. The two
women, politically and socially conscious, veteran fighters in
many good causes, were described in a review of the play in
the *Spectator* (March 28, 1958) as "oddly endearing amal-
gams" of Beatrice Webb and Molly Bloom. There is a sharp rift
between the mothers and the sons. The boys and girls of
twenty or so in the decade of the 1950's are totally uninterested
in politics, causes, demonstrations, and casual love affairs; security is what they want, and orderliness. The mothers are so anxious not to be possessive that they refuse to guide their sons. In
Act II, Milly having just returned from a trip to Japan with a
delegation of women, they discuss their sons. Myra had sent
Tony to a progressive school, hoping it would turn him into an
integrated personality, whereas Milly had sent Sandy to a public school, with the result that he has beautiful manners and
never does anything that is not calculated—he even falls in
love where it does him most good. She rather expected him to
drop her after completing his expensive education, but he
opted to stay with her. Why? One day she heard him say to one
of his "posh" friends, "You must meet my mother, she's such a
character." She obligingly played the role of a woman of the
people with a heart of gold: "I'll be an asset to him in the
Labour Party." Tony has long arguments with his mother;
when he listens to conversations between his mother and the
older men, he comments aside for the benefit of young Rose-

mary: "One half of this lot are bogged down emotionally in the thirties with the Spanish Civil War, and the other half came to a sticky end with Hungary."

At another point in the play Tony remarks to his mother: "I've spent a good part of what are known as my formative years listening to the conversation of the mature. . . . You're corrupt. You're sloppy and corrupt. I'm waiting for that moment when you put your foot down about something and say you've had enough. But you never do. All you do is watch things—with interest." Tony's notion of the vision his mother and her lot have created gives the play its title: "A house for every family . . . to every family a front door. . . . A house full of clean, well-fed people, and not one of them ever understands one word anyone else says. Everybody a kind of wilderness surrounded by barbed wire shouting across the defences into the other wildernesses and never getting an answer back. That's socialism. I suppose it's progress. . . . To every man his front door and his front door key. To each his own wilderness."

Tony, for all his cynicism about politics and causes, is a little Hamlet; he is emotionally upset by his mother's love affairs; he has grown up accustomed to "uncles." He clings to the house she owns—where all the happenings of the play take place—as a symbol of security; when he learns that she has sold it in order to have money to promote his career in anything he wants to do, he becomes hysterical. All he had wanted was to be with her in that house and to live with some sort of dignity; he was so tired of "all the brave speeches and the epic battles and the gestures." And his mother, bewildered, proclaims her own life a failure, since she had spent most of it bringing him up; but at least she had not been afraid to take chances and make mistakes. "The irony of it—that we should have given birth to a generation of little office boys and clerks and . . . little people who count their pensions before they're out of school." And off she goes—rather like Nora of A Doll's House—leaving young Rosemary wondering, "What's the matter with being safe—and ordinary?" and Tony saying, "Leave us alone to live."

When we meet Tommy in The Golden Notebook, we remember Tony. The son-mother relationship is explored on a deeper level, and the son finds a strange but convincing way out of his psychological impasse. To understand Tommy, it is not necessary to have met Tony in Doris Lessing's world, but it helps.

II *Free Women and Mothers*

A generation ago, Virginia Woolf, writing her feminist book, *A Room of One's Own*, was agreeably surprised to find among the first words of a new novel written by a woman that Chloe liked Olivia: "Sometimes women do like women." Chloe and Olivia share a laboratory as well as domestic interests. Doris Lessing's pairs—the two in the play and Molly and Anna in the novel—share politics and causes as well as domestic interests and the problems of motherhood. They are often together without any men around. "When women are alone," wrote Virginia Woolf, "unlit by the capricious and coloured light of the other sex," what are their gestures, their half-said words? And she noted how long accustomed women have been to concealment and suppression when they thought themselves observed. Looking back at the relationships between women in the English novel, she found them all too simple, with too much left out; women were shown almost always in relation to men. There is, continued Mrs. Woolf, a spot the size of a shilling in the back of the head, so they say, which no one can see for himself, and men for ages have pointed out to women that dark place at the back of their heads. A true picture of man as a whole cannot be painted until a woman has described to men that spot in the back of men's heads. Did Virginia Woolf do it perhaps in Mr. Ramsay—or Orlando? Has Doris Lessing done it with what some male reviewers consider her men victims in *The Golden Notebook?*

Developing her feminist theme, Mrs. Woolf recalled how women have sat indoors in many societies for millions of years, and how those rooms must have been permeated by woman's creative force. Doris Lessing's marked interest in rooms is not just the novelist's usual concern with background. An astonishing number of rooms in her world come to mind: that fascinating room of her childhood; the big living room in "Winter in July," with the African night outside; the cramped, shabby, suffocating little bedroom in *The Grass Is Singing* where Mary Turner slowly decays; the blitzed but cosy basement which Rose in *The Other Woman* hated to leave; Room Nineteen, where Susan drifts off down the dark river of her suicide; the swaying tower room of "Dialogue"; the spacious workroom where Anna's four notebooks—black, blue, red, and yellow— are spread out upon the long trestle table; and many others. In any search for symbolic meanings, here is a field for exploration.

The Golden Notebook opens with a conversation between Anna and Molly in the summer of 1957, after a separation. A review compared this opening with that of D. H. Lawrence's *Women in Love*, which is a dialogue between Ursula and Hermione. Lawrence, a rash man, was not afraid to set two young women talking together, unobserved. Doris Lessing's two women are close upon forty, and they are articulate upon all sorts of matters in a way that would have enraged Lawrence. Besides this opening conversation, there are three other brief sections of dialogue between them, each preceding extracts from the four notebooks, and a concluding conversation—five in all. It would not be amiss to put up a notice, "Danger! Free Women talking!"—like the warning at street excavations, "Danger! Men working!" For what these two experienced women say is often explosive.

"The two women were alone in the London flat." It is a sunny spring day, the windows are open, and men are delivering milk and selling fresh strawberries from the country in the street. Tommy, Molly's son, is in his room upstairs. It is a cheerful opening scene, but two reasons for uneasiness soon appear: Tommy is a problem, and Anna, with a successful first novel promising a literary career, seems unable to write. They eat strawberries and cream and drink wine in the sunlight, and catch up on what has happened to them during the year of separation. Richard, Molly's ex-husband and the father of Tommy, comes in and they discuss Tommy, who presently joins them. Richard is now married to Marion. It is a very cleverly constructed scene, with casually scattered clues to past events and future developments. As they remember and reflect upon their lives and opinions, the two women find many things rather odd. Molly is particularly sensitive to the oddity of things. At the end of the book, when Molly and Anna are looking at the roads ahead of them, it is Molly who says, "It's all very odd, isn't it, Anna?" And so it is, but continuously interesting, this story of "free women."

What, in the third quarter of the twentieth century, are the advantages, the opportunities, and the handicaps of women determined to be free? In 1929 Virginia Woolf specified a room of one's own and five hundred pounds a year for a woman writer. Wherever the income came from, it was to keep coming in without effort on the recipient's part. Anna has earned her income in the past; it derives from the royalties of her successful first novel; so, for a time at least, she can work at what she pleases, regardless of pay. Logically, it should be at another novel, but she has a "writer's block." As long as she is a member of the Party, she does volunteer work in the main office, reads the manuscripts submitted, and so on. When she leaves the Party, she is busy with her notebooks and with personal relationships that need a lot of attention. The sessions with her psychoanalyst alone must have taken up many hours. Molly, an artist in the theater, plays minor comedy parts. Her son, being grown, does not require the attention needed by Anna's little daughter. She has a house in London, in which Anna and Janet live until Anna takes a house of her own not far away, renting out a room when she can find a suitable tenant. One tenant, Ronnie, who figures in a vivid little episode with his homosexual friend, is very undesirable.

Other women in the novel include wives (there have to be wives so that there can be husbands to stray from home); a woman editor of a woman's magazine, a woman talent scout for the cinema, a woman worker in the Party office; but there are no women doctors or lawyers or teachers or members of Parliament. Since Virginia Woolf wrote *Three Guineas*, complaining of the narrow field for women's activity, women in the professions have greatly increased in numbers in England. The people Anna meets at parties or at work include interesting exiles from the Continent, an African or two, Americans in England for business or professional reasons, and American exiles—an export from the United States, thanks to the investigating activities of Congressional committees. The experiences Anna has with several of them lead her to generalizations about American men on this rather narrow personal basis. By having Anna working on a novel with a heroine named Ella, Mrs. Lessing introduces Ella's father, a retired army officer; Ella's lover Paul, a doctor; and several other characters. And by having Anna, though born and brought up in London, spend some of the war years in Southern Rhodesia, she can add Africa to the background, and Royal Air Force trainees and others to the cast.

Now what is it like to be "free and responsible, a woman in relation to men and other women, and to struggle to come to terms with one's self about these things and about writing and politics"—to quote from a *New Statesman* review of April 20, 1962? As for men, Molly and Anna "remain interested in men with a curiosity that is almost archaeological; as if there were so few good ones left that it is necessary to hunt for them amid the ruins," as Irving Howe writes.[1] Mr. Howe's comment is supported by one of Anna's observations: "I am always amazed in myself and in other women at the strength of our need to bolster men up. . . . Women have this instinctive need to build a man up as a man. . . . I suppose this is because real men become fewer and fewer." [2] At this point Anna is looking back on her life, realizing that a period of years shapes itself into a certain kind of being that can be rolled up and tucked away, or "named"; and being still within that period, one can foresee that, when it is over, one will glance back and say, "Yes, that is what I was." And the following quotation describes what Anna thinks she was at a moment of awareness that a new period was beginning which she must live through: "I was a woman terribly vulnerable, critical, using femaleness as a sort of standard or yardstick to measure and discard men. . . . I was an Anna who invited defeat from men without even being conscious of it. . . . I was stuck fast in an emotion common to women of our time, that can turn them bitter, or Lesbian, or solitary." (410) This estimate of herself is no mere statement;

her love affairs are acted out. But perhaps the most thought-provoking reflection about "free" women is simply this: "What's the use of us being free, if they [men] are not?"

Both Molly and Anna are responsible mothers. Molly's son Tommy is a problem, and his story develops within a complicated web of influences and counterinfluences, involving his mother; Anna; his father, Richard, important in the world of Big Business; and his father's second wife, Marion, whose friendship with Tommy brings about a very odd but credible solution for both his problem and hers. What happens to the children of "free" women? Tommy is one of the answers. His attempt at suicide leaves him blinded, and the blindness blocks off some of his troublesome complexes, leaving him a fragment of what he had the potentiality of being—but a self-consistent fragment. Fragmentation of the personality is a problem of our time along with alienation and loss of identity. Molly finds it very odd when her blind son becomes friendly with his father's second wife and they virtually take over Molly's flat: "My husband's second wife moving into my house because she can't live without my son. . . . I was sitting upstairs quiet as a mouse, so as not to disturb Marion and Tommy and thinking I'd simply pack a bag and wander off somewhere and leave them to it, and I thought that the generation after us are going to take one look at us, and get married at eighteen, forbid divorces, and go in for strict moral codes and all that, because otherwise the chaos is just too terrifying . . ." (435-36)

Anna's daughter is an anchor rather than a problem, and Anna is held back from going to pieces as long as she has to shape Janet's day from early morning to night into a healthy routine. It comes as a shock to the "free" woman that Janet, at thirteen, wants to go to the most conventional of boarding schools, wear an ugly uniform, walk in a "crocodile," and live the life depicted in vapid books about girls' schools. She seems destined by nature for an unproblematical life, this child of a mother who had no time for people "who haven't experimented with themselves, deliberately tried the frontiers." But Anna yields, and, when Janet goes, an Anna begins to come to life "who died when Janet was born."

III *Artist's Sensibility*

Anna's problem, her writing block, leads her obviously enough to a psychoanalyst. Of this interesting woman doctor, whom Anna and Molly call Mother Sugar, Mrs. Lessing draws a fascinating protrait. The sessions with her expose both private and public neuroses. Or, to quote Irving Howe again, Doris Lessing "grasps the connection between Anna Wulf's neuroses and the public disorders of the day." The connection is too much for Anna, and the novel is about how she cannot write a novel. On the last pages of *Remembrance of Things Past,* Proust's narrator begins to write the novel Proust has already written. Towards the end of *The Golden Notebook,* Anna's departing lover gives her the first sentence of the novel Doris Lessing has already written: "The two women were alone in the London flat." André Gide's alter ego, the novelist Edouard in *The Counterfeiters,* is living through his experiences and turning them into a novel at the same time. What is the relation between fiction and life? In the old days, as Sir Philip Sidney put it, the storyteller came with a tale that kept children from play and old men from the chimney corner. Now he comes with *Finnegan's Wake.* In an interview published in *The Queen,* Mrs. Lessing says: "If a writer writes a book like *Tom Jones,* and says 'Look at this young man,' it is quite a different thing from when, let us say, Jack Kerouac writes *On the Road.* He is saying, 'This is my sensibility, and it's what I believe in.'" [3]

Mrs. Lessing had other things to say in this interview. It is always worth while to listen to a writer's explanation of what he is trying to do, compare it with what he did, and perhaps discover that he did something else that even he himself did not know he was doing. Like many other novelists today, Mrs. Lessing has felt that the formal novel was not doing its job any more. So why not write the short formal novel and also put in the experience it came out of, and escape from that feeling writers have when they have finished a nice, tidy little book: "My God, that novel is supposed to be summing up all this!" Therefore, put in the short formal novel and *all this.* "I also split up the rest into four parts to express a split person. I felt that if the artist's sensibility is to be equated with the sensibility of the educated person, then it is logical to use different styles to express different kinds of people." The particular form she chose enabled her to say things about time, memory, and the human personality—"because personality is very much what is remembered; also it enabled me to say to the reader: Look, these apparently so different people have got so-and-so in common, or these things have got this in common. If I had used a conventional style, the old-fashioned novel, which I do not think is dead by any means . . . I would not have been able to do this kind of playing with time, memory and the balancing of people."

Doris Lessing, who has proved in many stories and novels that she can come to us quite simply with a tale, had reached the point when she was not satisfied with that. But embedded in the structure of *The Golden Notebook* are two tales equal to her best. Isn't it a little odd to remember that in the tradition of the English novel—a tradition which she says, in that interview, she is outside of—tales were introduced by Fielding and by Dickens in the most cheerfully obvious manner. If one has the storytelling gift, one will get the story in somehow. In the notebook with the black cover, Anna reviews experiences of her African years, and it is in these sections that two beautifully written episodes occur that could find a place in *African Stories*. I shall come back to them later.

The artist's sensibility as a mirror for our time has been explored by Proust, Joyce, Lawrence, Mann—the list is Mrs. Lessing's—and she calls this exploration one of the mainstreams of the modern novel. And to her Mann is the greatest. "If one were going to write after Thomas Mann who has said everything that can be said about the artist practising, what next? Mann's whole message was that art is rooted in corruption—in illness, above all." Mrs. Lessing thinks, however, that art is rooted in an overwhelming arrogance and egotism: "There is a kind of cold detachment at the core of any writer or artist." The artist has to be ruthless. But suppose he has a conscience about artistic creation? Tolstoy had, of course, because he came to the conclusion—at least as old as Plato—that artists are liars. But suppose one's conscience is concerned with being a good human being—what then? This viewpoint has crept into the socialist and communist attitudes to artists: "They say straight out or by implication that the writer has to serve society." A writer might be blocked by this kind of reasoning: "It's bad to spend my time writing books because I ought to be doing something about the state of the peasants somewhere. It's immoral to write when people are suffering." Such a writer could easily develop beautiful rationalizations for not writing. How far away seems the time when a Dickens had no doubt that he could tell his tales and at the same time expose the wrongs of society!

In the interview from which we have been quoting, Mrs. Lessing told about a woman she had known who wrote one highly successful novel and then could not go on, for reasons suggested by the above analysis. Asked how much society really entered into it, Mrs. Lessing replied, "I don't know. I merely used the writer's block to say something about a certain way of looking at the world." And, asked to sum up *The Golden Notebook* in a few sentences, she answered: "It is a novel about certain political and sexual attitudes that have force now; it is an attempt to explain them, to objectivize them, to set them in relation with each other. So in a way it is a social novel, written by someone whose training—or at least whose habit of mind—is to see these things socially, not personally."

Doris Lessing, with an impressive list of books to her credit, is not suffering from a writer's block. So she cannot be identified with Anna Wulf, except in so far as Anna's creator, with her insight into many of Anna's emotions and attitudes, can imagine a writer being blocked by them. Are they her own emotions and attitudes? This is a tricky question for critics, and Mrs. Lessing expressed irritation with a review in the *Times Literary Supplement* which equated Martha Quest with Doris Lessing, and then compared Martha Quest with Anna Wulf, presenting the two women as combinations of the author and her characters. But it isn't surprising for a reader or even a critic to become perplexed about the character-creating process. Three leading characters in *War and Peace* were imaginatively projected out of the rich many-sided personality of Tolstoy—Andrey, Pierre, and Nicholas. Each resembles Tolstoy in certain basic characteristics and experiences, but this obviously did not bother Tolstoy. But suppose that Nicholas Rostov, created by Tolstoy as Anna was created by Doris Lessing, decides to write a novel about Ivan X. And this Ivan begins by resembling Nicholas, but then takes on a different identity; and Nicholas becomes self-conscious about what is going on in himself. Doris Lessing launches Anna Wulf into *The Golden Notebook*, and Anna decides to write a novel about Ella. "I see Ella, walking slowly about a big empty room, thinking, waiting. I, Anna, see Ella. Who is of course, Anna. But that is the point, for she is not. The moment I, Anna, write: Ella rings up Julia to announce, etc., then Ella floats away from me and becomes someone else. I don't understand what happens at the moment Ella separates herself from me and becomes Ella." (393) Well, who does?

One of the truths about Anna at this stage is that she is going to pieces. It is the author's intention that she should go to pieces, but not to the point of suicide—only to the point of devastating self-knowledge. Anna's preoccupation with social problems comes from the kind of education (in the Western world), vaguely humanistic, in which it is assumed that "everything is for the best, justice will prevail, that human beings are equal, that if we try hard enough, society is going to become perfect, that people are fundamentally good. These are attitudes that seem increasingly absurd in the world as it is now." The absurdity may become, however, more than one can stand. Mrs. Lessing seems to believe that these humanistic attitudes, good in themselves, can swing over into their opposite and become profoundly destructive. Anna becomes split by the conflict within her; the split is symbolized by the four notebooks— the African memories, the experience with Communism, the diary, and the short novel. The possible fusing together of the fragmented parts in a new whole is symbolized by the golden notebook, which, oddly enough, Anna gives to her last or latest lover, who is even more divided within himself than she is. One of the briefly summarized story ideas in the novel outlines this situation: "Same theme as Chekhov's *The Darling*. But this time the woman doesn't change to suit different men, one after another; she changes in response to one man who is a psychological chameleon, so that in the course of a day she can be half a dozen different personalities, either in opposition to, or in harmony with him." (461-62)

In the last of the yellow notebook entries, of which the first three have been devoted to the novel about Ella, Ella has disappeared, and, instead of a coherent narrative, there are nineteen fragments of possible stories, of which the above quotation is one. Then follows Anna's diary in the blue notebook, recording among other things the course of her affair with an American, Saul Green. This affair seems to contain in embryo many of the stories. Just why Mrs. Lessing puts the story ideas first and then follows with the experience out of which they might have come, isn't clear, but the sequence convinces the reader that Anna's confusion is pretty serious. Dates, in other parts of the book carefully noted, are omitted. Saul Green has no sense of time when he is in some of his chameleon phases, and Anna appears to have joined him. A group of paragraphs, numbered 1 through 18, each headed with the phrase "a short story" or "a short novel," appears in the yellow notebook. It is as if Anna had read through it, seeing eighteen possible stories. Or did she jot down the story ideas first, and then have the stages of the affair to order? She may know how to transform fiction into life. She does dream to order while undergoing psychoanalysis. These dreams are remarkable. Some of them recall the nightmares of destruction recorded in *Going Home*. They are also developing dreams in sequence, as in that delightful story, "Two Potters." In one of the latest, when Anna is nearest to a complete breakdown, a tiger appears, quite a memorable beast. He turns up during her disastrous love affair with Saul Green, and the tiger image is used again in Mrs. Lessing's drama, *Play with a Tiger*. There is nice hunting here for the explicators of symbols.

IV *Nightmares and Obsessions*

What are some of Anna's nightmares and obsessions? Several of them are also Martha Quest's. Martha was haunted by the specter of repetition, of being part of a cycle, of being her mother over again, and of repeating the experience of generation after generation. That specter takes shape after she is married and feels trapped. Much earlier, when a young girl, she experienced a timeless moment of complete depersonalization. She was walking home at sunset from an errand at the station, a white girl alone on the veld, an unusual experience in itself. The natural beauty around her induced a mood of ecstatic union with nature, for which she was prepared by her absorbed reading of English poetry. "The bush lay quiet about her, a bare slope of sunset-tinted grass moved gently with a tiny rustling sound. . . . She stood quite still, waiting for the moment, which was now inevitable. There was a movement at the corner of her eye," and a small buck came out from the trees and stood quietly flicking its tail a few paces away. "The buck gazed at her; and then turned its head to look into the bush, laying its ears forward. A second buck tripped out from the trees, and they both stood watching her; then they walked daintily across the ground, their hooves clicking sharp on the stones, the sun warm on their soft brown hides. They dropped their heads to graze, while their little tails shook from side to side impatiently, with flashes of light." The feeling in Martha deepened: "There was a slow integration during which she, and the little animals, and the moving grasses, and the sunwarmed trees, and the slopes of shivering, silvery mealies, and the great dome of blue light overhead, and the stones of earth under her feet, became one, shuddering together in a dissolution of dancing atoms." During a brief space of time—"which was timeless"—she understood quite finally "her smallness, the unimportance of humanity. In her ears was an inchoate grinding, the great wheels of movement, and it was inhuman, like the blundering rocking movement of a bullock cart." What it meant continued to perplex her in memory. (*Children of Violence,* 61-63)

In one of Anna Wulf's sessions with Mother Sugar, Anna, rejecting the remedy for pain that consists in putting it away where it cannot hurt by turning it into a story or into history, declares herself convinced that there are whole areas of herself made by the kind of experience women have not had before. Mother Sugar smiles. "Never?" And behind her voice Anna hears the sounds always evoked at such moments—"seas lapping on old beaches, voices of people centuries dead." Mother

Sugar insists that the details change but the form is the same; she calls up the artist-women, the independent women of the past who insisted on sexual freedom, a line stretching back into history. But Anna argues that they did not look at themselves as she does or feel as she does. "I don't want to be told when I wake up terrified by a dream of total annihilation, because of the H-bomb exploding, that people felt that way about the cross-bow. It isn't true. There is something new in the world. . . . I don't want to be told when I suddenly have a vision . . . of a life that isn't full of hatred and fear and envy and competition every minute of the night and the day that this is simply the old dream of the golden age brought up to date. . . . The dream of the golden age is a million times more powerful because it's possible, just as total destruction is possible. Probably *because* both are possible. . . . I want to be able to separate in myself what is old and cyclic, the recurring history, the myth, from what is new, what I feel or think that might be new . . ." (403-404)

If she meets a man who is cracked, split across, it might mean, Anna thinks, that he is keeping himself open for something. She is not satisfied, as she accuses Mother Sugar of being, if she recognizes in a dream this or that myth or folk tale and has thus gone beyond the childish, transmuted it, and saved it by embodying it in a myth. She is not satisfied to fish among her childish memories and to merge them with the art or ideas that belong to the childhood of a people. In this process "the individual recognizes one part after another of his earlier life as an aspect of general human experience." But does he become free when he can say that what he did or felt is "only a reflection of that great archetypal dream, or epic story, or stage in history?" He has separated himself from the experience, or fitted it like a piece of mosaic into a very old pattern. Is he then free of the individual pain of it? Anna is not convinced.

Anna's obsession with repetition plays a part in her decision to leave the Communist party. Toward the end of her five-year affair with Michael, she tries to assess the quality of her life by writing down as truthfully as she can every detail of one day, say the 17th of September, 1954—a literary project that has tempted many since Joyce wrote *Ulysses* and Virginia Woolf, *Mrs. Dalloway*. She notes physical details with the power to shock—again reminiscent of Joyce. Then she realizes that we deal with physical aspects of living quite without conscious thinking, almost as we breathe; but start writing them down, and the balance between truth and fact is shifted. She spends the day at the office of the Party, in informal and formal conferences, talking freely with several of the workers, old and young, whom she knows best, realizing that some of this talk would be accounted treasonable in a Communist state; yet realizing, too, that, when she leaves the Party, she will miss "the company of people who have spent their lives in a certain kind of atmosphere, where it is taken for granted that their lives must be related to a central philosophy."

She has understood that the Communist party, like any other organization, "continues to exist by a process of absorbing its critics into itself. It either absorbs them or destroys them." But on this day she sees the process rather differently. There is the group of hardened, fossilized men, that is opposed by fresh young revolutionaries; they form between them a balanced whole until the young in their turn become the hardened and the fossilized, and a group of fresh, lively-minded, critical people send forth shoots of new life. But the old and sapless are kept in existence for some time. No right, no wrong, "a process, a wheel turning." And though everything in Anna cries out against such a view of life, it has the power to throw her back into a political-terrorist nightmare, which she relates with spine-chilling clarity and which owes much to the actual memories of her lover Michael—memories of relatives murdered in gas chambers, of close friends, Communists, who were murdered by Communists. (293-95)

One of the duties of this day in the Party office is to decide whether or not to publish some manuscripts, politically correct but artistically bad, as the committee well knows; but they are "healthy" art. Anna is aware of her inconsistency in rejecting her own fiction as unhealthy and also rejecting "healthy" art when she sees it. Here is another block. But Anna is not blocked when she indulges herself in the writing of parodies or *pastiche* of the healthy Communist story, of the African story (*Blood on the Banana Leaves*), or of the avant-garde stories in American little magazines. She gives up in sheer disgust because what is actually published is itself parody. At a later stage of her breakdown, she forces herself to contemplate the horrors and absurdities and ironies of current history by tacking up on the walls of the room where her notebooks are spread out on the long trestle table newspaper headlines and clippings about the world's hideous disorders. This is a very effective device for inducing hysteria—one not to be recommended.

V *The Film Sequence*

In the section entitled "The Golden Notebook," almost at the end of the novel, Anna, looking back over her life, sees it in film sequences run off by a projectionist, and names each as it appears: the Mashopi film; the film about Paul and Ella; the film about Michael and Anna; that about Ella and Julia; that about Anna and Molly—all directed by Anna Wulf. And Anna is faced by the burden of recreating order out of the chaos her life has become. "Time had gone, and my memory did not exist, and I was unable to distinguish between what I had invented and what I had known, and I knew that what I had invented was all false. It was a whirl, an orderless dance, like the dance of the white butterflies in a shimmer of heat, over the damp sandy vlei."

The Mashopi film belongs to the period during the war when Anna Wulf spent the years 1939-1945 in Salisbury, Southern Rhodesia. One wonders how Anna, born in a house in Baker Street, London, came to be in Salisbury, where she had married and divorced Max Wulf, a shadowy figure. In the Mashopi episodes, Anna is Willi Rodde's girl, and Willi is a Communist refugee from Hitler's Germany. It is always a pleasure to have Doris Lessing back in Africa; and if she wishes to put Anna Wulf there, though Anna, unlike Martha Quest, did not grow up there, that is fine. The result is the Mashopi film, unrolled in two sections of the black notebook, and some of her most brilliant writing. (55-135; 353-72)

Recalling her African experiences, Anna writes: "In our own small town a year after Russia entered the war, there had come into existence a small orchestra, readers' circles, two dramatic groups, a film society, an amateur survey of the conditions of urban African children, and half a dozen discussion groups on African problems." For the first time the town enjoyed something like a cultural life, shared by hundreds who knew Communists only as people to hate. The little group of Communists, though they had inspired these activities, often paradoxically disapproved of them, but "a dedicated faith in humanity spreads ripples in all directions." People who do not even know it have been inspired or given a new push into life because of the Communist party. The tiny group in the colonial capital had no links at all with such African movements as there were, but operated in a vacuum, so that its debates and conflicts were internal; and within a year the group was split, equipped with splinter groups, with traitors, and with a loyal hard core that kept changing, except for one or two at the very center.

Several members of the group go for week ends to a country hotel about sixty miles from the town, at a small station called Mashopi: Willi Rodde, authority on Marxism; Anna Wulf; the beautiful Maryrose from a Cape family; and three young Englishmen in training at the Royal Air Force base. Paul and Jimmy are both from Oxford and Ted is from the London working class. Paul has great charm but a hidden arrogance that often leads him to malicious mockery of unsuspecting people; his is a class arrogance. Willi is equally arrogant in his intellectual certainties, and the two are antagonistic, but attracted to each other and very much alike. Jimmy, a homosexual, is hopelessly devoted to Paul, who does not respond except with irritation. To Maryrose, her brother, recently killed, had been a little more than kin. Ted Brown, a genuine Socialist, is always rescuing some promising young man from darkness. Paul is in love with Anna, and everybody is in love with Maryrose, who is friendly to them but can love no one but the lost brother. "We were all at various times in love with each other," as Paul said; it was obligatory in the times they lived in to be in love with as many people as possible. Anna tries to remember just what each was like. She draws up parallel columns of contradictory traits in Willi's character, but falls back on the fact that we remember someone we have known by a trick of gesture, a smile, a look, that seems to hold the essence of his personality. Personality is a unique flame. Anna would agree with D. H. Lawrence, who once wrote: "I conceive of a man's body as a kind of flame, like a small candle flame, forever upright and yet flowing." [4]

The group quarreled on these week ends over Communist tactics. They considered "black nationalism" a right-wing deviation, and only once, as Anna recalls, did they come anywhere near the truth, and "that was when Paul spoke in a spirit of angry parody," foretelling developments not unlike those in Kenya a decade later. "All this while the ox-wagons rolled by in the white dust of the sand-veld, the trains rocked by on the way from the Indian Ocean to the capital, while the farmers drank in their khaki in the bar, and groups of Africans, in search of work, hung around under the jacaranda tree, hour after hour."

The hotel was right in the bush, complete with kopjes and natives, but also with an English bar, dart boards, steak and kidney pie, and the Boothbys to run it—Mrs. Boothby an ex-barmaid, and Mr. Boothby an ex-sergeant-major. The servants were of course natives, and the cook occupied a privileged position, being allowed to live on the grounds with his family. A frequent visitor was an older man, George Hounslow, an inspector of the railroad, who had for his mistress the cook's wife and whose conscience was oddly disturbed by his half-caste baby. Trouble grew out of this situation and out of Paul's making friends with the cook; that sort of thing just wasn't done, and it worried Mrs. Boothby, who liked Paul. The cook was as puzzled as Mrs. Boothby. But, with the colony full of air force men from outside, many Africans had become aware that a white man could treat a black man as a human being. A moving part of the story is the unhappy outcome for the cook and his family.

Other visitors to the hotel were the local farmers and trainees of the nonintellectual variety, such as Johnny, a gifted jazz pianist, and Stanley, who kept him supplied with cigarettes and beers so that he would not stop playing. Mrs. Lattimer, middle-aged but beautiful and promiscuous, attracted Stanley;

her husband took it out on her when he was drunk. There were dances and festivals, several love affairs got under way, and one of them ended in disaster, as Anna remembers; but actually what was painful about that time was that nothing was really disastrous. "It was all wrong, ugly, unhappy and coloured with cynicism, but nothing was tragic, there were no moments that could change anything or anybody. From time to time the emotional lightning flashed and showed a landscape of private misery and then—we went on dancing." All this time her own group organized meetings, discussions, and debates; read and argued; cured souls and helped people; and they earned their livings. The men being trained were under continuous nervous strain, and they all lived at this pitch for over two years, becoming slightly mad out of sheer exhaustion.

These memories of Mashopi occur in the pattern of the novel, the pattern Mrs. Lessing chose (as quoted above) because she wanted to say things about time, memory, and personality that did not fit into the neat structure of the well-made novel. The memories are not consecutive; the two main episodes are widely separated. Bits of them may turn up in dreams. The second episode comes back to her after she dreams of an incident on a London street when a man in a hurry kicked and killed a pigeon. Even in the dream she had struggled to recall what that had reminded her of. When she woke, she recaptured it in clear detail, and she was exasperated to realize—as we all do sometimes—that our brains contain so much that is locked up and unreachable until some trivial incident unlocks it. What she recaptured is a treasure of beauty and insight.

Because of the earlier recollections of the week ends at the hotel, we already know the characters in the little drama and the tensions that exist among them. Mrs. Boothby suggested one pleasant morning after a heavy rain that, if one of the boys could shoot, he could take Mr. Boothby's rifle, go to a spot not far from the hotel where pigeons were likely to congregate, and shoot enough of them for a pigeon pie. So Paul, who remarked in his bantering manner that his expensive education had not failed to include the niceties of grouse and pheasant murder, took the rifle; he collected Anna and Maryrose,

Willi and Jimmy, and they set forth. Willi carried along *Stalin on the Colonial Question*. Because of the heavy rain the night before, there was now a festival of insects—a riot of white butterflies in the air, and on the grass and over the road millions of brightly colored grasshoppers.

They paused to watch the insects coupling: "the happy or well-mated insects stood all around us, one above the other, with their bright round idiotic black eyes staring." It was absurd, obscene, fascinating. Better to watch the butterflies, but they too were pursuing vile sex, as Paul remarked, not just celebrating the joy of life. Jimmy and Paul interfered with the grasshoppers, seeking with grass stems to persuade the ill-mated to regroup themselves into well-matched couples; the scientific approach, said Paul with satisfaction, admiring his rearrangement; but the insects soon changed back into their old positions. Jimmy saw no evidence that "in what we refer to as nature things are any better ordered than they are with us" and perhaps in this "riot of debauchery" males were with males, females with females. Paul, irritated, stepped on the couples he had organized. Anyway, all these insects would be dead by night. If they weren't, if they didn't kill each other and weren't eaten by birds, they would bury the hotel under a crawling mass, and swarms of butterflies would dance a victory dance over the deaths of Mr. and Mrs. Boothby and their daughter. This led to talk about the prodigality of nature and to analogies with human societies; when Paul said, "The point I was trying to make, comrades," Willi, the father-figure in the group, interrupted: "We know the point you are trying to make . . . let's go and get the pigeons."

Anna remembers them, five brightly colored young people, walking with the sun stinging their backs, in the grassy vlei, through "reeling white butterflies under a splendid blue sky." They settle down in a shady spot at the foot of a kopje, "a giant pile of pebbles," to await the coming of the pigeons. The kopje is "full of the earthworks and barricades built by the Mashona seventy, eighty years before as a defense against the raiding Matabele. It was also full of magnificent Bushmen paintings." Paul imagines a war scene as savage as the insect wars. A pigeon coos nearby; he shoots it down, and then remarks that "we need a dog to fetch it"—and Jimmy is the dog. Later Paul looks with distaste at a wounded pigeon and says, "Do you expect me to kill the thing in cold blood?" But this time Jimmy waits for Paul to prove himself; the pigeon obligingly dies first. The drama between Paul and Jimmy plays itself out along with the shooting of the pigeons and the battles between an anteater in the bottom of a sand pit and the victim ants and beetles. Meanwhile Willi reads steadily on, the corpses of the pigeons accumulate, and there is a smell of blood.

A file of natives, farm workers, passes on the track nearby, talking and laughing, but falling silent and averting their faces when they see the white group. And this introduces the colonial problem. Here in the little colonial society, on "this insignificant handful of sand on the beaches of time," a million and a half blacks and one hundred thousand whites exist to make one another miserable, when there is enough of everything, including talent, "to create light where darkness now exists." And why? Willi comes out with an answer so exactly what the others expect that they burst out laughing: "There is no need to look any further than the philosophy of the class struggle." They revert to the Mashona-Matabele days when men fought for land, women, food—for good reasons, not like us. "As a result," Paul predicts, "of fine comrades like Willi, ever ready to devote themselves to others, or people like me, concerned only with profits, I predict that in fifty years all this fine empty country we see stretching before us filled only with butterflies and grasshoppers will be covered by semi-detached houses filled by well-clothed black workers." Willi sees nothing the matter with that, and Jimmy, serious as ever, cannot see why the houses need to be semi-detached, for under Socialism. . . . The conversation is interrupted by a deadly fight between the anteater and a beetle, both disappearing under the sand, which heaves and eddies in "a suffocating silent battle." One of the group comments: "If we had ears that could hear, the air would be full of screams, groans, grunts, and gasps. But as it is, there reigns over the sun-bathed veld the silence of peace." They go back to the hotel with their bag of pigeons. "Our heads ached with the heat. We were slightly sick with the smell of blood."

In the brilliantly depicted African landscape and in an atmosphere heavy with the menace of war, the tensions—sexual, emotional, intellectual—among the three men and two women are dramatized in dialogue and action, stimulated by their half-reluctant and half-fascinated interest in the pigeon-shooting and in the life and death struggles of the insect world.

When Anna, living in a kind of nightmare, watched the film sequences of her life unroll themselves, she saw the Mashopi hotel explode in "a dancing whirling cloud of white petals or wings" of the butterflies which had chosen to alight on the building:

It looked like a white flower opening slowly, under the deep steamy blue sky. Then a feeling of menace came into us, and we knew we had suffered a trick of sight, had been deluded. We were looking at the explosion of a hydrogen bomb, and a white flower unfolded under the blue sky in such perfection of puffs, folds and eddying shapes that we could not move, although we knew we were menaced by it. It was unbelievably beautiful, the shape of death; and we stood watching in silence, until the silence was slowly invaded by a rustling, crawling, grating sound, and looking down we saw the grasshoppers, their gross tumbling fecundity inches deep, all around us. (528)

This pattern of images, repeated with variations, conveying both beauty and terror, helps to shape a novel that is complex, far-ranging, often difficult, fragmented like our society and our consciousness, challenging in its art and its ideas.

CHAPTER 6

Attitudes and Influences

I FEEL," Mrs. Lessing is quoted as saying in the interview published in *The Queen* in 1962, "the best thing that ever happened to me was that I was brought up out of England. I took for granted kinds of experience that would be impossible to a middle-class girl here." She recalls the contrast Virginia Woolf had pointed out in *A Room of One's Own* between the restrictions that hemmed in Charlotte Brontë, the English governess, and the freedom to explore all possibilities that was open to Tolstoy, the Russian aristocrat, during the same period. Some of these restrictions still affected women in England in Virginia Woolf's day, as she herself pointed out in both her frankly feminist books, *A Room of One's Own* and *Three Guineas*. Mrs. Lessing feels that Virginia Woolf's experience must have been too limited, "because there's always a point in her novels when I think, 'Fine, but look at what you've left out.'" But, one may comment, there is no need to infer limited experience from what a writer may choose to leave out. Nevertheless, growing up in Southern Rhodesia was very different from growing up at Hyde Park Gate. It meant a freedom to explore the veld with dog and gun that recalls Emily Brontë's freedom of the Yorkshire moors. And so we have in Mrs. Lessing's fiction the African landscape, the overarching African sky, the African wild life, and above all the colonial color problem.

Another point Mrs. Lessing makes in the interview is that she considers her writing to be outside the English tradition. She never felt really close to the English novel, "whereas I feel so close to the Russian novel that it's as if they were all my blood brothers." But she is closer to the English novel than she realizes in this sense of kinship with the great Russians. It is no news at this late date that the influence of Tolstoy, Turgenev, Dostoevsky, and Chekhov was very strong indeed on some of the leading English and American writers, from the late nineteenth century on. The influence of Turgenev on Virginia Woolf and on Henry James is an instance. In discovering the Russians, through their literature, to be blood brothers, the young reader in Southern Rhodesia was responding to a fascination that had become almost a commonplace by the time she was born in 1919. "I've always read the Russians as if they were me and the English as if they had nothing to do with me, except for Thomas Hardy, the Brontës, and Dickens." Dickens is admitted in spite of "the nonsense he writes about women." She explains that it is "this English attitude towards women" that she dislikes so much in so many novels. Turning from literature to life, she criticizes, "with one or two honourable exceptions," the entire British middle-class male population: "Something happens to them, I don't know what it is, probably the public schools or something, but they just baffle me. They don't know anything about women. The working class are quite different—they actually like women." The expression of that bafflement is in Mrs. Lessing's novels, for all to read and ponder.

George Eliot is not included among the English novelists who had something to do with Mrs. Lessing, and this is odd, for at times—especially in the Martha Quest novels—the psychological analysis is very much in George Eliot's manner: sober, penetrating, with the note of authority, and sometimes overcareful to leave nothing obscure or unrelated to life. Martha herself is a Rhodesian white colonial Maggie Tulliver: rebellious, adventurous, romantic, chafing against the barriers of a narrow provincial society, and deeply influenced by books. The following passage is an example of the George Eliot manner. Martha, perplexed by some of the problems of her new marital status, goes to the bookcase for help:

Books. Words. There must surely be some pattern of words which would neatly and safely cage what she felt—isolate her emotions so that she could look at them from outside. For she was of that generation who, having found nothing in religion, had formed themselves by literature. And the books which spoke most directly were those which had come out of Western Europe during the past hundred years, and of those, the personal and self-confessing. And so she knelt in front of a bookcase, in driving need of the right arrangement of words, for it is a remarkable fact that she was left unmoved by criticisms of the sort of person she was by parents, relations, preachers, teachers, politicians and the people who write for the newspapers; whereas an unsympathetic description of a character similar to her own in a novel would send her into a condition of anxious soul-searching for days. Which suggests that it is of no use for artists to insist, with such nervous disinclination for responsibility, that their productions are only "a divine play" or "a reflection from the creative fires of irony," etc., etc., while the Marthas of this world read and search with the craving thought, What does this say about my life? It will not do at all—but it must be admitted that there always came a point where Martha turned from the novelists and tale tellers to that section of the bookcase which was full of books called *The Psychology of . . . , The Behaviour of . . . , A Guide to . . .* , with the half-formulated thought that the novelists had not caught up with life; for there was no doubt that the sort of things she or Stella or Alice talked about found no reflection in literature—or rather, it was the attitudes of mind they took for granted that did not appear there, from which she deduced that women in literature were still what men, or the men-women, wished they were. In this other part of the bookcase, however, were no such omissions; she found what she was thinking and feeling described with an admirable lack of ambiguity. (*A Proper Marriage,* 321-22)

Martha's search for literary guidance in life, cooperating with her instincts and the customs of her social group, takes her into fields of sexual experience that the Victorian novel abstained from exploring. Mrs. Lessing explores them with, to borrow her phrase, "an admirable lack of ambiguity." One wonders what George Eliot, Charlotte Brontë, and Olive Schreiner would have thought of the result. Would they have found more congenial to their literary taste the fantastic sexual experiences of Virginia Woolf's Orlando? A triumph of ambiguity?

Mrs. Lessing early in her career chose the straight, broad, direct style of narrative—a style that would be familiar to a devoted reader of the great nineteenth-century novelists. She writes in that style in most of the fiction we have discussed, up to *The Golden Notebook*. There she had things to say that required a departure from the formal novel, and she tried to find a shape that would contain them. She did not experiment for the sake of experimenting, as critics at first supposed Virginia Woolf to be doing in *Mrs. Dalloway;* what actually happened to Mrs. Woolf was that, when the idea of *Mrs. Dalloway* came to her, it began to create a house for itself, without conscious direction. Doris Lessing must have had some such experience.

In an interview recorded in 1963 by Roy Newquist and published in *Counterpoint,* Mrs. Lessing talks of the different levels of awareness inside of us, and of the moments when a writer feels he has hit one of these levels. A certain kind of writing or emotion comes from the experience. It was very frightening to write a story like "To Room Nineteen"—a story soaked in emotions that she did not recognize as her own. How could she write about a boredom so intense that the victim commits suicide, when she doesn't understand how people can be bored? Once, just for the experience, Mrs. Lessing tried the drug mescaline, and during the four or five hours under its influence she was aware of many levels. Different "I's" played their parts. She was both a mother giving birth and the baby being born, and yet she was neither. The baby was a philosophic infant, who argued steadily with God, and was yet bored with a boredom quite different from that of the woman in "To Room Nineteen." It was a cosmic weariness; it was exhaustion in advance at the thought of going through it all again, for the baby had been born many times. Mrs. Lessing gives Martha Quest and Anna Wulf glimpses of this cosmic boredom, characterized by a horror of repetition, the feeling of ancient seas lapping on old beaches. They do not succumb to this weariness; and even in the mescaline experience the bored philosophic infant continues to argue steadily with God.

Mrs. Lessing does not need a drug to reach another level. When she wrote *The Golden Notebook,* she tells us, she deliberately evoked the different levels to write different parts of it: "To write the part where two characters are a bit mad, I couldn't do it. I couldn't get to that level. Then I didn't eat for some time by accident (I forgot) and found that there I was." The fascination of establishing contact with different levels of consciousness might draw some novelists more self-absorbed than Mrs. Lessing into a closed private world. With her, however, to judge from *The Golden Notebook,* it is more likely to enrich the essentially social and realistic pattern of her fiction. The world is very much with her. She is deeply committed to the humanism of the nineteenth-century classics: the warmth, the compassion, the love of people, which makes these old novels a statement of belief in man.[1]

For a time she was depressed because she thought it likely that the novel might be on its way out altogether—born of the middle class, it might die with it. But the novelist has one advantage denied to many other artists: the novel is the only popular art form where the artist speaks directly in clear words to his audience; "the novelist talks as one individual to individuals—in a small personal voice."[2] Mrs. Lessing's personal voice speaks out of the experience of having been brought up at the center of a modern battlefield, in a society undergoing rapid dramatic change. She saw the cruelties of the white man toward the black man as one of "the heaviest counts in the indictment against humanity." But she has also come to see color prejudice as "only one aspect of the atrophy of the imagination that prevents us from seeing ourselves in every creature that breathes under the sun."[3] Africa is more to her than a battleground:

I believe that the chief gift from Africa to writers, white and black, is the continent itself, its presence which for some people is like an old fever, latent always in their blood; or like an old wound throbbing in the bones as the air changes. That is not a place to visit unless one chooses to be an exile ever afterwards from an inexplicable majestic silence lying just over the border of memory or of thought. Africa gives you the knowledge that man is a small creature among other creatures, in a large landscape.[4]

Mrs. Lessing has pictured the African landscape and peopled it with creatures from beetles and ants to men and women, black and white. She has also made us free of London streets and London flats, and will continue, one is confident, to expand our horizons and keep our imaginations from becoming atrophied. As a disciplined dreamer, waking or sleeping, she

has probably played the game ascribed to her Anna Wulf—
a game that might symbolize the ambition of a novelist. Anna
used to play this game in her childhood, at night before going
to sleep:

First I created the room I sat in, object by object, "naming" every‚
thing, bed, chair, curtains, till it was whole in my mind, then move
out of the room, creating the house, then out of the house, slowly
creating the street, then rise into the air, looking down on London,
at the enormous sprawling wastes of London, but holding at the
same time the room, and the house and the street in my mind, and
then England, the shape of England in Britain, then the little group
of islands lying against the continent, then slowly, slowly, I would
create the world, continent by continent, ocean by ocean (but the
point of "the game" was to create this vastness while holding the
bedroom, the house, the street in their littleness in my mind at the
same time) until the point was reached where I moved out into
space, and watched the world, a sunlit ball in the sky, turning and
rolling beneath me. Then, having reached that point, with the stars
around me, and the little earth turning underneath me, I'd try to
imagine at the same time, a drop of water, swarming with life, or a
green leaf. Sometimes I could reach what I wanted, a simultaneous
knowledge of vastness and of smallness. Or I would concentrate on
a single creature, a small coloured fish in a pool, or a single flower,
or a moth, and try to create, to "name" the being of the flower, the
moth, the fish, slowly creating around it the forest, or the sea-pool,
or the space of blowing night air that tilted my wings. And then,
out, suddenly, from the smallness into space. (*The Golden Notebook*, 469)

Notes and References

Chapter One

1. *Manchester Guardian,* May 13, 1960.
2. *New Statesman,* June 4, 1960.
3. *Sunday Times* (London), June 5, 1960.
4. *Hudson Review,* Summer, 1961, pp. 289 ff.
5. *Evening Standard* (London), June 14, 1960.
6. *Daily Post* (Liverpool), June 1, 1960.
7. *John O'London's,* July 7, 1960.

Chapter Two

1. Preface, *African Stories.*

Chapter Three

1. The volumes in which the stories discussed in this chapter appear can be identified in the Bibliography.

Chapter Four

1. Page references are to the Prometheus Books paperback edition.
2. Page references to quotations from *Martha Quest* and *A Proper Marriage* are to the *Children of Violence* edition. (Simon & Schuster)
3. The party is described in pages 305 to 320.
4. This episode is described in pages 159 to 175, *A Ripple from the Storm.*

Chapter Five

1. *New Republic,* December 15, 1962.
2. *The Golden Notebook,* p. 414. Page references to this novel are from the edition published by Simon & Schuster (New York, 1962).
3. *The Queen,* August 21, 1962.
4. Letter to Ernest Collings, January 17, 1913. *Letters of D. H. Lawrence,* Viking Press. P. 96.

Chapter Six

1. "The Small Personal Voice," in *Declaration.*
2. *Ibid.*
3. Preface, *African Stories.*
4. *Ibid.*

Selected Bibliography

PRIMARY SOURCES

I. *Novels and Stories (listed in the order of publication)*

The Grass Is Singing. London, Michael Joseph, 1950; Penguin Books (paperback), 1961; Ballantine Books (paperback), New York, 1964.

This Was the Old Chief's Country. London, Michael Joseph, 1951. Ten short stories, all with African settings: "The Old Chief Mshlanga," "A Sunrise on the Veld," "No Witchcraft for Sale," "The Second Hut," "The Nuisance," "The De Wets Come to Kloof Grange," "Little Tembi," "Old John's Place," " 'Leopard' George," "Winter in July."

Martha Quest. London, Michael Joseph, 1952; New York, Simon & Schuster, 1964 (in *Children of Violence*).

Five. London, Michael Joseph, 1953; Penguin Books, in association with Michael Joseph (paperback), 1960. Five short novels: *A Home for the Highland Cattle, The Other Woman, Eldorado, The Antheap, Hunger.* Received the Somerset Maugham award in 1954 as the best literary work of the year by a British author under thirty-five. See also *African Stories.*

A Proper Marriage. London, Michael Joseph, 1954; New York, Simon & Schuster, 1964 (in *Children of Violence*).

"Myself as Sportsman." *The New Yorker,* January 21, 1956. First-person sketch about learning to hunt with a rifle in Southern Rhodesia; it has not so far been reprinted.

Retreat to Innocence. London, Michael Joseph, 1956; New York, Prometheus Books (paperback), 1959.

The Habit of Loving. London, MacGibbon & Kee, 1957; New York, T. Y. Crowell Co., 1957. Seventeen short stories: "The Habit of Loving," "The Words He Said," "The Woman," "Through the Tunnel" (first published in *The New Yorker,* August 6, 1955), "Lucy Grange," "Pleasure," "A Mild Attack of Locusts" (first published in *The New Yorker,* February 26, 1955), "The Witness," "Flavors of Exile," "Getting Off the Altitude," "A Road to the Big City," "Flight," "The Day Stalin Died," "Plants and Girls," "Wine," "He," "The Eye of God in Paradise."

A Ripple from the Storm. London, Michael Joseph, 1958. The third novel in the series *Children of Violence,* to be followed by *Landlocked* (not yet published) and a fifth volume; the entire series to be published by Simon & Schuster.

The Golden Notebook. London, Michael Joseph, 1962; New York, Simon & Schuster, 1962; New York, McGraw-Hill (paperback), 1963); London, Penguin Books (paperback), 1964.

A Man and Two Women. London, MacGibbon & Kee, 1963; New York, Simon & Schuster, 1963. Nineteen short stories, of which several appeared first in English and American magazines, including *The New Reasoner, The New Statesman, Encounter, Partisan Review, Kenyon Review, Views:* "One off the Short List," "The Story of Two Dogs," "The Sun between Their Feet," "A Woman on a Roof," "How I Finally Lost my Heart," "A Man and Two Women," "A Room," "England versus England," "Two Potters," "Between Men," "A Letter from Home," "Our Friend Judith," "Each Other," "Homage for Isaac Babel," "Outside the Ministry," "Dialogue," "Notes for a Case History," "The New Man," "To Room Nineteen."

African Stories. London, Michael Joseph, 1964. Two early stories, "The Trinket Box" and "The Pig," are here printed for the first time; "The Black Madonna" appeared in *Winter's Tales* (Macmillan, 1957), and "Traitors" in *Argosy,* May, 1954. The ten short stories in *This Was the Old Chief's Country* are reprinted and the four novelettes in *Five* with an African setting; *The Other Woman* is omitted. There is a preface by the author.

Children of Violence. New York, Simon & Schuster, 1964. Vol. I, *Martha Quest;* Vol. II, *A Proper Marriage.*

II. *Personal Narratives*

Going Home. London, Michael Joseph, 1957. Drawings by Paul Hogarth. Account of Mrs. Lessing's return visit to Rhodesia in 1956, dedicated to "good friends, both in London and Central Africa, white and black, who helped me during my trip, and while writing the book, with time, money, experience and advice."

In Pursuit of the English. London, MacGibbon & Kee, 1960; New York, Simon & Schuster, 1961. The author's experiences in London after she left Southern Rhodesia in 1949; the narrative comes close to being a novel, its interest centering in a rooming house and its tenants.

III. *Plays*

Each His Own Wilderness, in *New English Dramatists, Three Plays,*
introduced and edited by E. Martin Browne. London, Penguin
Books (paperback), 1959. The three plays are *Each His Own
Wilderness;* Bernard Kops, *The Hamlet of Stepney Green;* and
Arnold Wesker, *Chicken Soup with Barley.* The introduction
states that *Each His Own Wilderness* was produced at the
Royal Court in London, March 23, 1958, by the English Stage
Society.

Play with a Tiger: A Play in Three Acts. London, Michael Joseph,
1962. First produced at the Comedy Theatre, London, March
22, 1962. Included are the author's notes on directing the play,
which was written in 1958.

Mr. Dolinger. Not published, but produced early in 1958 at the Oxford Playhouse.

The Truth about Billy Newton. Not published, but produced, running for a fortnight at a theater in Salisbury, England, in 1961.
(Letter from Doris Lessing, April 1, 1964.)

IV. *Articles and Interviews*

"Being Prohibited," *New Statesman,* April 21, 1956.

"Karuba Project," *New Statesman,* June 9, 1956.

"London Diary," *New Statesman,* March 15 and 22, 1958.

"The Small Personal Voice," in *Declaration.* London, MacGibbon
& Kee, 1957. A collection of "separate positions" by eight con-
tributors, including Doris Lessing, Colin Wilson, John Osborne,
John Wain, Kenneth Tynan, Bill Hopkins, Lindsay Anderson,
and Stuart Holroyd. Doris Lessing's statement is on pp. 13-27.

"Crisis in Central Africa," *Twentieth Century,* CLXV (April, 1959).
Three articles devoted to the New Africa, by Nadine Gordimer,
William Plomer, and Doris Lessing. Doris Lessing's article is on
the theme of "white supremacy," the essence of which is "hum-
bug." She recalls a scene she witnessed when she was a girl,
between a white farmer and a native laborer, which left her
with a "sense of improbability that has never left me since."

"Footnote to the Golden Notebook." Interview with Doris Lessing
by Robert Rubens, in *The Queen,* London, August 21, 1962.

"All Seething Underneath," *Vogue* (New York), February 15, 1964.
Reminiscences of her father by Doris Lessing.

Interview by Roy Newquist, October, 1963, in London, in *Counterpoint,* Rand McNally & Co. (New York, Chicago, San Fran-
cisco, 1964), pp. 414-25.

"Zambia's Joyful Week," *New Statesman,* November 6, 1964. Mrs. Lessing describes the celebration of Zambia's independence, at Lusaka, the capital of the new African state, formerly Northern Rhodesia.

V. *Poems*

Fourteen Poems. London, Scorpion Press, 1959. Limited to 500 copies.

SECONDARY SOURCES

I. *Books*

GINDIN, JAMES. *Postwar British Fiction.* University of California Press, 1962; Cambridge University Press, 1963. Contains a chapter on Doris Lessing, as "a committed writer."

KARL, FREDERICK. *A Reader's Guide to the Contemporary English Novel.* New York, Farrar, Strauss & Cudahy, 1962; London, Thames & Hudson, 1963. Contains a few pages of comment on Doris Lessing, especially on the Martha Quest novels.

II.

Book reviews and articles in English and United States magazines and newspapers, selected for their value as critical appraisals of Doris Lessing's works, and listed under the titles, chronologically arranged, of her works

The Grass Is Singing

CHURCH, RICHARD. *John O' London's,* March 17, 1950.

JOHNSON, PAMELA HANSFORD. *Daily Telegraph* (London), March 14, 1950.

LASKI, MARGHANITA. *Spectator,* March 31, 1950.

Times Literary Supplement, April 14, 1950.

WHITE, ANTONIA. *New Statesman,* April 1, 1950.

WYNDHAM, FRANCIS. *Observer,* March 19, 1950.

This Was the Old Chief's Country

LASKI, MARGHANITA. *Observer,* April 22 and December 30, 1951.

SNOW, C. P. *Sunday Times* (London), April 8, 1951.

SPRING, HOWARD. *Country Life* (London), April 20, 1951.

STREET, ALLEN. *Current Literature* (London), April, 1951.

STRONG, L. A. G. *Spectator,* May 4, 1951.

Selected Bibliography

SYMONS, JULIAN. *Manchester Evening News,* April 12, 1951.
WINTRINGHAM, MARGARET. *Time and Tide,* July 28, 1951.
A Proper Marriage
  AMIS, KINGSLEY. *Spectator,* October 8, 1954.
  DAVENPORT, JOHN. *Observer,* September 26, 1954.
  MARSHALL, ARTHUR CALDER. British Broadcasting Corp., December 12, 1954.
  Times Literary Supplement, October 22, 1954.
The Habit of Loving
  FULLER, ROY. *London Magazine,* March, 1958.
  HEINEMANN, MARGOT. *Daily Worker* (London), January 2, 1958.
  JOHNSON, PAMELA HANSFORD. *New Statesman,* November 23, 1957.
  KLEIN, MARCUS. *Hudson Review,* Winter, 1958-59.
  MICHAELIS-JENA, RUTH. *Weekly Scotsman,* January 11, 1958.
  SYMONS, JULIAN. *Evening Standard* (London), November 19, 1957.
  Times Literary Supplement, November 29, 1957.
A Ripple from the Storm
  Times Literary Supplement, October 24, 1958.
Each His Own Wilderness
  BRIEN, ALAN. *Spectator,* March 28, 1958.
  WORSLEY, T. S. "The Do-gooders," *New Statesman,* March 29, 1958.
In Pursuit of the English
  FINDLATER, RICHARD. *Evening Standard* (London), June 14, 1960.
  GILLIATT, PENELOPE. *Spectator,* May 20, 1960.
  John O' London's, July 7, 1960.
  JONES, MERVYN. *Observer,* May 8, 1960.
  LAMBERT, G. W. *Sunday Times* (London), June 5, 1960.
  LASKI, MARGHANITA. *News Chronicle* (London), May 11, 1960.
  MAIR, L. P. *Listener,* May 26, 1960.
  MUDRICK, MARVIN. *Hudson Review,* Summer, 1961.
  ROSSELLI, JOHN. *Guardian,* May 12, 1960.
  Times Literary Supplement, May 19 and July 1, 1960.
  WARE, JEAN. *Liverpool Daily Post,* June 1, 1960.
  WATERHOUSE, KEITH. *New Statesman,* June 4, 1960.
The Golden Notebook
  BLIVEN, NAOMI. *The New Yorker,* June 1, 1963.
  BOWMAN, SYLVIA. *News-Sentinel* (Fort Wayne, Indiana), June 30, 1962.

BRITTEN, ANNE. "Doris Lessing's Whirlwind," *Books and Bookmen*, May, 1962.

BROOKS, JEREMY. "Doris Lessing's Chinese Box," *Sunday Times* (London), April 15, 1962.

DOLBIER, MAURICE. *New York Herald-Tribune*, June 29, 1962.

EMERSON, JOYCE. *Bookman*, May, 1962.

FRUCHTER, NORMAN. *Studies on the Left*, Spring, 1964.

HICKS, GRANVILLE. "Complexities of a Free Woman," *Saturday Review* (New York), June 30, 1962.

HOPE, FRANCIS. "Heroine of Our Time," *Observer*, April 15, 1962.

HOWE, IRVING. "Neither Compromise nor Happiness," *New Republic*, December 15, 1962.

MOORE, HARRY T. *Herald* (Boston), July 1, 1962.

NORDELL, RODERICK. "Theme & Technique," *Christian Science Monitor*, July 5, 1962.

NOTT, KATHLEEN. "Counterpoint to Lawrence," *Time and Tide*, April 26, 1962.

TAUBMAN, ROBERT. "Free Women," *New Statesman*, April 20, 1962.

Times Literary Supplement. "The Fog of War," April 27, 1962.

WATSON, W. H. C. "Up Against the Wall," *The Scotsman*, April 21, 1962.

WHITE, ELLINGTON. *Kenyon Review*, Autumn, 1962.

A Man and Two Women

KAUFFMANN, STANLEY. "The World is Much with Her," *New York Times Book Review*, October 13, 1963.

SCHOTT, WEBSTER. "The Purpose of Life," *Nation*, December 14, 1963.

TAUBMAN, ROBERT. "Near Zero," *New Statesman*, November 8, 1963.

WARDLE, IRVING. "Happiness Isn't Allowed," *Observer*, October 6, 1963.

Children of Violence

BERGONZI, BERNARD. "In Pursuit of Doris Lessing," *New York Review*, February 11, 1965.

HOWE, FLORENCE. "Doris Lessing's Free Women," *Nation*, January 11, 1965.

III. *Social and political background of Rhodesia*

MASON, PHILIP. *The Birth of a Dilemma*. Oxford University Press, 1958.

Index

Index